Dalcamo Funeral Home
470 W. 26th St.
Chicago, IL 60616
(312) 842-8681

Family owned & operated
Serving the families of
Bridgeport since
1939

Bernard M Dalcamo
&
Matthew F. Dalcamo Fr.

PREFACE

These neighborhood stories were formulated in my mind throughout my entire life: as an observer or a participant; interviewing or researching; looking back or reporting a then current event for articles that I wrote for the Bridgeport News, the Chicago Sun Times, the Chicago Tribune, the Gazette and the South Loop's "the new city."

Wonderment starting with my youth:

> Remembering the day WWII ended; watching neighbors tearing up newspapers and throwing the pieces like confetti into the air.

> Commercial buildings had unfamiliar names or long-ago dates under the cornices—what civilizations had gone before? I often wondered.

> Working at the family's real estate office only heightened my interest in historic structures as well as the people who occupied them.

Instead of studying law, I majored in English at De Paul University. (I'm sure that my parents, especially my father, understand now looking down, as I sound like the Big Bad Wolf: "the better to describe it all My Dears.")

> "You want to interview me?" the surprised and humble barber will ask in "Sonata in G on Morgan Street".

> "Yes," I answered assuredly, for that story that is in all of us.

Within these pages, walk our streets, enter our homes—the hearts of our people; enjoy my salad days up to a mind turned philosophic. Welcome to My Bridgeport.

John E. Aranza

Acknowledgement

My son John D. Aranza, who prompted me to compile my writings into this book and not let a dream remain just a dream.

My wife Elaine, patient as all wives are.

My Sponsors, whose participation supported this publication and have faith in our community. Please Support them.

A special thanks to Larry Mooney who continually offered more assistance, and especially Jerry Moran (You didn't think I'd let this pass
unheralded?) owner, Popeye's Chicken, 3204 S. Ashland, 773-254-2200, who assisted me greatly, offered more, and refused to have an ad placed.

People like these & the Dalcamos, Cacciatore, Harris, Filbert's, Mike Pilkington's Bridgeport Coffee Co., Dr Schwartz, Punky's and the generations of families and friends that make up Bridgeport and Armour Square, - you have always nurtured and inspired me.

John E. Aranza

Cover: Standing, left to right. My father, John Aranza (1891-1962); sister, Mary Condic Aranza (Ageless); Joan Aranza (1930-1955); mother, Anna Billich Aranza (1908-1990); In the grass, sister, Phyllis Cafferty Aranza (1935-) and your author, John E. Aranza (1939-)

A History That…Time Forgets

There's a hundred-mile ribbon in the hair of Illinois prairie grass—the Illinois and Michigan Canal. And deservedly, the Illinois and Michigan Canal National Corridor is being formulated in Congress. In effect, a National Park for the entire canal along its course into mid-Illinois through an evocative litany of historical towns and areas: Channahon, Ottawa, and La Salle; McKinley Forest, Goose Lake Prairie, and Starved Rock.

years would pass before its completion: the time needed for a primitive civilization to mature; for Wars of Independence and Indian hostilities to end.

In 1830, a surveyor ironically named James Thompson began platting the canal in a swampy area inhabited by 50 people at the southwest corner of Lake Michigan. The Canal Commissioners also assigned him to plat future towns at either end of the canal:

The abandoned I&M Canal used as a dumping ground. Ca. 1930. This section under the Stevenson Expressway (as all of the Canal is up to Harlem Avenue) looking west from approximately Kedzie Avenue.

Yet in the hard tasks of our everyday lives, we haven't had the time to herald our neighborhood's story: that Bridgeport's history began with the canal.

It was conceived by Louis Joliet in 1674 after he explored our region with Marquette—a water route from Lake Michigan to the Gulf of Mexico, beginning with a canal from the Checagou River. But over 160

Bridgeport was platted then too. Construction of the channel began in 1836, and Bridgeport was annexed to the town at the northeast terminus whose population has grown to 4,000; mostly on speculation that the site then named Chicago might achieve prominence.

The canal was opened in 1848 and when it

By John Aranza 3

An idyllic young boy's scene. My son, John D. Aranza, gazing at the canal's terminus in Justice, Illinois.

quickly the years can obscure it. Standing where Fuller Street ends on the east bank of the Chicago River, you can meditate on an explorer's idea whose fruition gave birth to our community. You can imagine the sounds of the picks and shovels of unknown laborers etching out the soil for the canal's route 140 years ago.

Fuller Street was Bridge Street then, and so named because it was extended by a bridge across the river to a pumping station at the mouth of the canal. (The bridge is no longer there, but across from the original inlet of the canal can still be seen between the Enterprise paint factory and the service station north of it.) Lock Street was and still is named for the canal locks that were at the terminus there. (Perhaps they are only covered by landfill and not removed?) Eleanor Street, still next to you, was called Water Street, and it also ran across the river parallel to Ashland Avenue where the fishery is now.

Looking at the Loop in the distance and its rectangular skyscrapers that rise in a cluster like Disney's Magic Kingdom, you could lament that its glitter and the Gold Coast north of it began because of what's for-

earned $159,000 in tolls in 1871—the year it fully paid its construction indebtedness—the population of the city named after the wild onions growing along the river had exploded to 300,000.

Other modes of transportation, however, replaced the canal's usefulness. At the start of 1848, Chicago had no trains; six years later it was the railroad center of the world.

And when the larger Sanitary and Ship Canal (a continuation of the South Branch of the Chicago River) was opened besides it in 1900, the canal's commercial use ceased. Allowing its headwaters to silt up, it lay fallow in Chicago for over 60 years. Finally, it was laid to rest in an unmarked grave beneath the Stevenson Expressway (I-55) without a tombstone where it originated at the Chicago River at Ashland Avenue. Such is Sandburg's Chicago, I thought:

"Building, breaking, rebuilding…"

Bridgeport's heritage is prominent, yet how

…and the author meditating at the same site. Ca. 1983

gotten here. But that's the other side of the fence, isn't it?

What we have—the ethnic heritage of our work; of hard-earned homes and carefully attended gardens and equally cared for children—shouldn't be overlooked either. Maybe in that National Corridor process, recognition will be given to this site along the river; to our neighborhood within the city.

Or is there something we can do now? So while occasionally forgetting, it won't be entirely forgotten? Our history must be remembered.

- From The Gazette -

Forgotten heroes: Bridgeport and Armour Square's World War II veterans

Time has a cruel and sad way of erasing memories and shrouding the past in forgetfulness.

As much as we are a loving people, our present everyday problems obscure the accomplishments of those who shaped our neighborhoods and our country, especially our World War II veterans. They are worth remembering this Veterans' Day. Although there are a few old commemorative pillars in the neighborhood and a stone at 34th and Aberdeen Streets, World War II vets are not honored with a neighborhood square, statue, or museum. They are our overlooked heroes.

"Most of us were sons of immigrants who answered the call to defend the country without protest," said Milenko Burazin concerning himself and his fellow World War II veterans from the Bridgeport and Armour Square areas. They were "proud to be accepted into the armed forces."

Then a 20-year-old private first class, Burazin

was in the first wave of the invasion force on Okinawa on April 1, 1945. Wounded and hospitalized, he re-

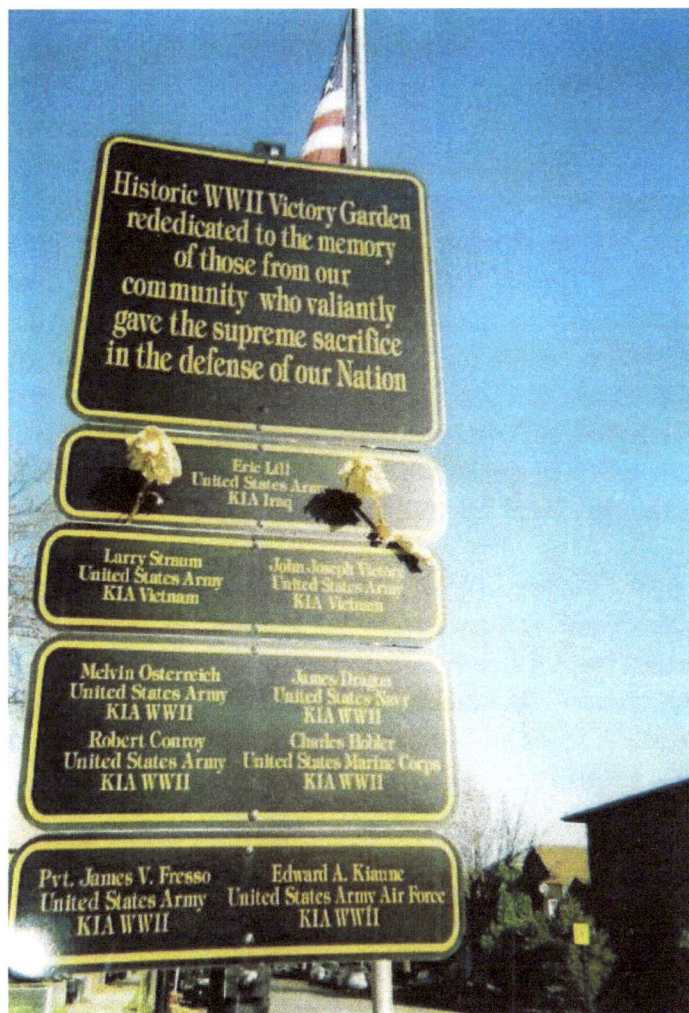

11th Ward Alderman, James Balcer, a decorated Viet Nam Veteran, sponsored a replacement memorial at 30th and S. Canal St (aka Victory Gardens) because flowers were placed around them. (He also had restored the concrete Star base of the flag pole at 29th and S. Normal)

ceived a Purple Heart medal. His mother learned of his injuries by watching him being carried on a stretcher in a theatre newsreel. He recovered and was given further duties as part of the first force to occupy Japan immediately after the bombings that ended the war, entering Tokyo Harbor on Aug. 27.

After fighting on Iwo Jima, another Bridgeport-Armour Square resident followed him into Japan with the occupation forces: Michael Bilandic, who in the 1970s would become Chicago's Mayor.

Ultimate Sacrifice

Burazin and Bilandic came home, but the men from the Koestner family, who lived at 34th Street and

By John Aranza 5

Wallace Avenue, made the ultimate sacrifice, and their family suffered greatly. All Army servicemen, George Koestner was killed in Alaska in May 1943, Michael Koestner in Italy in November 1943, and Henry Koestner in France in November 1944.

The remains of Cpl. Edward Maciejewski were brought back 60 years after his death. A member of the elite Marine Raiders, he was shot by a sniper in 1942 on the Japanese-held Makin Atoll. His and the graves of 17 of his buddies were found in 2000. A man who, as a boy, had helped bury The Marines led an Army expedition to them. Cpl. Maciejewski eventually was reinterred at Arlington National Cemetery. The heroism of his group of soldiers was depicted in the 1943 Randolph Scott movie "Gung Ho."

In June of 1945, Cpt. Aloysius Mezydlo of 28th and Quinn Streets was killed at Camp Wheeler, CA, retrieving a fragmentation grenade two trainees threw, which had bounced back at them. After 1 month in the North African and Italian campaigns, he ended up getting killed stateside.

Married while on leave in June 1945, Joseph Gorecki of 33rd and Aberdeen Streets was declared missing in action after the sinking of the U.S.S. Indianapolis. In September his bride, Gertrude, received the crushing news from the War Department that there was no hope for his survival.

George "Red" Landre fared better. He was retrieved miraculously from the treacherous North Sea after being swept overboard. John Condich of St. Jerome's Parish survived parachuting behind enemy lines at Normandy during the D-Day invasion.

The Real Iwo Jima story

The most unheralded event of World War II was the little known original flag raising on Iwo Jima, with James Michael of 2811 South Emerald Avenue in the foreground, guarding his buddies from enemy snipers in nearby caves. His daughter, Betty McMahon recalled his stories of boats sounding whistles and sirens in the surrounding waters while men were cheering. It was the first raising of the American flag on Japanese soil. A photo was taken for Leatherneck Magazine. Hours later , a battalion officer ordered the first flag taken down so a second, planned raising could be pho-

tographed by the Associated Press. That pictured was wired back to America and seen by the world.

McMahon expressed the wish that someone who knew Stephen Spielberg or Clint Eastwood would contact them to put this obscure fact in a movie. Eastwood is planning a movie for Spielberg's Dream-Works Studio about a Battle of Iwo Jima, a film based on the writings that refer only incidentally to this fact. Do life and fate have to close chapters so unceremoniously?

Lack of Ceremony

For many returning vets, lack of ceremony was the order of the day. John Kohlmann of 29th and Wallace Streets, a waist gunner armorer, flew 50 missions over Europe, shooting out of an open, side by window of a B-24 in freezing temperatures. He returned home on a Friday in late 1945 and went back to his old job the following Monday.

It is time for permanent records and memorials of neighborhood servicemen and women of all wars-a living repository, not just a museum. It should include a collection of our neighborhood pride, histories of all of our ethnic groups" and churches, with visuals such as photos and artifacts. It should be staffed and open for viewing, research, and discussion.

If anyone has a store to donate for this purpose or wants to contribute. contact this writer at the Gazette.

Let us not let this idea fade. Our neighborhood heritage is too precious for someone in the future not to be able to know who the people were who lived here and what they accomplished.- The Gazette

Proud mothers at another Victory Garden unveiling.

Names on the Honor Roll

Edward Fahey	Huburt Durkin
Vito Starzdas	John Sproule
Anthony Florio	John McNamara
Walter Dobrovolski	Stanley Bielowski
James Maker	Raymond Eteionne
Frank Dobrovolski	William Connors
Francis Connors	John Murphy
Edward Lafin	James Haggan
Joseph Balsomo	Frank Melewski

Don and Bob Shinnick, Nativity of Our Lord's Steeple in the background at 37th and Union. Sears and Montgomery Ward patriotically offered children's uniforms in their catalogues.

Jack Murphy standing in front of his neighborhood's Honor Roll Memorial near 37th and South Halsted. Notice how he replicates the saluting figure!

28th and S. Wallace Streets. Newlywed Greg Sintic was killed in Viet Nam in 1968. Eddie Walz and I coached him and his Saint Anthony's basketball team. I lent him my car for his Prom. We all have our memories and losses, I know.

36th and S. Wallace Streets. Lt Joseph T. (Jay) McKeon Jr. was killed in Viet Nam in 1967. The family's funeral home is located at 37th and Lowe.

By John Aranza 7

CHICAGO PARK DISTRICT

IN MEMORY OF SEAMAN 1ST CLASS JAMES E. HUMBERT
BORN APRIL 13, 1924 - KILLED IN ACTION JANUARY 10, 1945
ABOARD THE U.S.S. LE RAY WILSON D.E. 414, LINGAYEN ATTACK FORCE PHILIPPINES

WHEN THE SHIP, ON WHICH HE WAS THE GUNNER OF A TWENTY MILLIMETER ANTI-AIRCRAFT GUN, WAS ATTACKED BY A JAPANESE BOMBER DURING EARLY MORNING TWILIGHT ON JANUARY 10, 1945. HE IMMEADIATLEY TOOK THE ENEMY PLANE UNDER FIRE AND KEPT IT UNDER FIRE UNTIL IT CRASHED INTO HIS GUN STATION. HIS ACCURATE FIRE INFLICTED DAMAGE TO THE PLANE, CAUSING IT TO SWERVE FROM A COURSE THAT WOULD HAVE INFLICTED GRIEVOUS DAMAGE TO HIS SHIP. HIS CONDUCT IN THE FACE OF CERTAIN DISASTER UNDOUBTEDLY RESULTED IN THE SAVING OF A LARGE NUMBER OF LIVES AND PREVENTED THE INFLICTION OF HEAVY DAMAGE TO HIS SHIP. FOR HIS HEROIC ACTION, ABOVE AND BEYOND THE CALL OF DUTY, HE IS HEREBY AWARDED THE "NAVY CROSS".

I DO NOT LOOK UPON THE SUICIDE ATTACK ON OUR SHIP AS BEING A SINGLE ACTION, BUT RATHER AS A TRAGIC CLIMAX OF A SERIES OF ENGAGEMENTS DURING WHICH THIS SHIP BY THE GRACE OF GOD AND THE EXCELLENCE OF IT'S GUNNERS HAD ESCAPED INJURY. THE ACTION OF HUMBERT AND ALL THE REST IS MORE HEROIC WHEN IT IS REMEMBERED THAT THEY HAD SEEN MANY OTHER SHIPS SUBJECTED TO THE SAME TYPE OF ATTACKS, AND KNEW AND APPRECIATED THE EXTREME DANGER OF THEIR POSITION AND THE UNLIKELIHOOD OF THEIR ESCAPING WITH THEIR LIVES AT THE MOMENT OF THE ATTACK. THE EXPRESSION THAT "HE ACTED IN KEEPING WITH THE HIGHEST NAVAL TRADITIONS" IS AN EXPRESSION OFTEN FREELY USED, AND ONE THAT IS SOMETIMES, PERHAPS, TOO LIGHTLY USED, WHEN WE THINK OF THE VALOROUS DEEDS OF OUR NAVAL HEROS WHO HAVE GONE BEFORE. WITH THAT THOUGHT IN MIND I DO NOT SAY THAT HUMBERT ACTED IN KEEPING WITH THE HIGHEST NAVAL TRADITIONS, I SAY THAT HE MADE NAVAL TRADITION. MAY HIS GALLANT ACT LIVE ALWAYS IN THE MEMORY OF A GRATEFUL NATION. MAY ADMIRAL KILAND KNOW, WHEN HE READS THIS REPORT, THAT HE KEPT HIS FAITH IN HIM. HE WAS MY SHIPMATE AND I AM PROUD OF HIM.

M.V. CARSON, JR. - COMMANDING OFFICER USS LE RAY WILSON D.E. 414

| SILVER STAR | PURPLE HEART | LIBERATION PHILIPPINES | ASIAN PACIFIC | EURO-AFRICAN EAST CAMPAIGN | AMERICAN CAMPAIGN | WW II VICTORY |

(Robert Humbert, brother, life-long Bridgeport resident, related: "Admiral Killian of the Fleet Command issued an Order that under an enemy attack , gunners could not leave their stations '... until relieved from duty by the Angel of Death or the Vail of the Unconcious.' Unlike others who left theirs during a suicide assault , my brother did not run but stood by his gun. When checked later , it was empty of ammo . Badly burned , he died while beeing transfered to the Hospital Ship Cambria and was later buried at sea".)

The Old Neighborhood Italian American Club members and neighborhood families perpetualized, Armour Square and Bridgeport Veterans in front of their club house on S. Shields Ave between 30th & 31st Streets.

Memorial at 34th and Aberdeen sponsored by the Bridgeport VFW Post 5079 .

"Loose lips might sink ships" was a World War II slogan to remind citizens back home and soldiers in the theater to keep their mouths shut to avoid inadvertent leaks. The pamphlet given to soldiers included warnings like this: "A harmful letter can be nullified by censorship; loose talk is direct delivery to the enemy."

T.WAC Gazette.

Published Monthly | August 1943 | Vol. I

?????????? AND JUST EXACTLY WHO ARE THEY ??????????

Most likely you are wondering who we are and may think we sound a little waccy. Well we may not be in the service of Uncle Sam but we are trying to do our bit on the home front, as the "Travelers' Women's Auxiliary Club," formed to keep the home fires burning, while YOU serve Uncle Sam.

At the beginning of last March, 17 Travelers were in service, leaving but 11 to carry on; so something had to be done to keep the club in tact. At a special meeting the fellows decided to call upon the girls for help.

On March 8th, a joint meeting was held at which time the TWACS were originated. There are now 8 girls in the club and in due time we hope to expand. In order that you may once again enjoy these good old times at the club we will do our best to maintain it. Just like the WACS, we are only for the duration.

Marilyn Hurley Laidley-Pres.
Loretta Schweihs, Sec. & Treas.
Loretta Dingles
Emily Gallinetti
Hilda Gallinetti
Teresa Horvath
Rose Augle Mossman
Irene Tampier

The TWACS Gazette started for the purpose of keeping YOU informed about your fellow members also serving Uncle Sam, as well as other neighborhood news. The only possible way to make this paper a success is for YOU to let us in on what you are doing. Send all information to the club

3045 Normal Avenue

*****

DID YOU KNOW THAT!---

Pvt. Bill (Red) Mossman and Rose Augle were married; Wednesday April 21, 1943 at All Saints Church. Ted Hoard was best man.

Rose has now deserted the TWACS to be with her husband who is stationed in Alabama.

*****

Since March Joe Dub left fro the Army Air Corps, and is now stationed in Missouri.

*****

Bob Koestner, Member of the Army Air Force is in training at Fresno, California.

*****

Willard Cole, is in the engineering division of the Army. Stationed at Colorado Springs, Colo.

*****

Corp. James (Sende) [illegible]eidersberg was home on a twenty-one day furlough from Newfoundland in June.

GERONIMO!

THE LITTLE RED FOX

Red Mossman, who is in France,
writes that he is OK, although
seeing combat. "My only prayer
is that this mess is over and
mighty fast.
It's getting so I'm about to
ask for jump pay. I jump in
my fox hole so much you would
think I was a paratrooper.
I received your paper and I
was looking forward to seeing
it for a long time, so when
it came I was really happy!
I don't mind the days over here,
but after 11, its time for
the Luftwoffe." Hope you'll
soon be having music put you
to sleep nights, Red!
It surely is encouraging to
hear so many of you say you
enjoy the Gazette. Such favor-
able response makes writing
the paper much more fun.

All of you please write often, if you want an interesting paper.
to read!!!

A postal, portraying a picture of
St. Peter's Basilica in Rome,
comes from Brent Murray. He
writes--"Had the chance to
see Rome sometime ago and went
to Holy Communion at St Peter's-
It's a beautiful city, but I'll
take peacetime and Chicago any
day.
Things are good and the boys
still write about Steve's
chile being used in hand-grenades."
The TWAC'S have often heard
about Steve's but so far we've
never tried the food, thanks
for the tip, Brent.
****

HELP!! HELP!! HELP!!

THE GAZETTE DEPENDS

UPON ITS FRIENDS

NO - NO - ANYTHING BUT THAT!

CHILI

HOT TIME IN BERLIN.

From the Archives of Teresa Horvath Lara : The club was formed to write neighborhood friends in the Service of happenings back home and to publish their letters back from them . Since there was censorship by the War Department to all correspondence so not to reveal American positions, the second page illustrates the general light-heartedness of them; and probably also to bouy spirits . The first floor of the building at 3045 South Nornal was rented by the group as an Office and Clubhouse for the duration of the War .

OVERDUE OVERTURE

By JOHN ARANZA
special to *the new city*

It was a different kind of parade. A different kind of army. A different kind of veteran. No neat rows of pressed uniforms and polished boots, precisioning like the Radio City Rockettes.

They were the continental Army. Wounded. Some rumpled and troubled-looking. No longer boys, yet not middle aged either. Yet something of both.

I watched from the corner of Jackson and Dearborn, far from the LaSalle Street reviewing stand. But the reactions here were just as intense.

As if cheering long-distance runners nearing a finish line, the crowd applauded the first approaching group of loosely-cadenced marchers—in camouflage shirts and worn jeans, or regulation pants and jean jackets; in complete field dress, looking as if just worn in combat. A few raised beer cans to salute the crowd. But most were decorated with rows of ribbons, bars and medals.

Then many cried when they realized that the parade was led by a legless vet on a mechanic's crawler, propelled by boxing-type gloves as he grinned and pounded on the street, pulling himself forward.

For nearly hours, the clapping only stopped when the parade slackened. The vets walked to the curbs and shook as many hands as possible. Quickly, stories were told of being spit at when returning home in the '70s. "Thank you Chicago, Thank you America."

"Thank you! Welcome Home. Welcome Home." was heard continuously.

A banner on the Dirksen Federal Building read: VETERANS: ONE GOOD JOB DESERVES ANOTHER.

Marchers' read: OUR MIA'S NEVER FORGOTTEN. PRAISE THE WARRIOR, NOT THE WAR. PEACE. FLORIDA. MICHIGAN. IOWA.

I thought of grainy films I've seen all of my life, Of Paris' Liberation, and waving, crying Frenchmen, of the end of WW II, and snake-dancing Loop crowds.

And this.

Faded stars being recognized, before it was too late. I'm certain that the crowd thought of it too.

Their cheering was never mechanical, like for a perfunctory curtain call. It was loving, sorry-sounding, not trying to match the protests years before, no matter who was right.

The war's themes and symbols came to mind: drug use, Pacifism, Heroism, Napalm, casualties, unrecognizable goals and enemies and only now this process of justification, healing. I felt sorry and glad for every one there, but for all who were in Vietnam, for the physical and mental wounds that perhaps will always be their reminders—no parade, I thought, though so sympathetically deserved, no medals, no words, no testimonials could ascribe as much as their most excrutiating feat in what only they know and alone can say, that THEY SERVED.

By John Aranza 11

Other Thoughts

The absolute last stop of our vacation that I mentioned last week was to visit my uncle John Bilic. Driving back from any trip, I would always go to his place at Spectacle Lake, Indiana. He's dead now, and instead of his summer cottage that he made into a year-round home, we go to St. Paul's, a country cemetery three blocks south of Route 30 and the campus of Valparaiso University.

But it's really three million miles from earth on one of those little side roads you see outside of Anywhere, USA leading nameless off the state highways, usually dividing a cornfield, and making you wonder what is out there away from civilization.

An iron archway leads into the cemetery, and there is no fencing around it at all. His grave is about twenty feet from an embankment, and a railroad track is behind him; I'm sure jostling him as those who live behind the C&WI on Canal Street.

Rather than feel depressed, I find comfort there. And in more somber moods, I sometimes feel that there are more good people among the dead than are living.

They don't cause hurts; we lionize them into grander proportions than they were; but the ones we really miss are so because the quality that was theirs is gone from our lives, cannot be found again, and will not touch us any more.

I use to see Eugene Pellegrini of 30th and Parnell on solitary walks in the neighborhood before he died. I'm sure that he had the freshness of all youths, but I only knew him as an adult and he was a quiet, sad-appearing man to me. His expression was one of personal anxiety: of some deep-felt emotion he was reflecting on.

Rather than punctuate his conversation with "God forbids" or "Gob Bless yous," he seemed to sense the meanness of life more than the rest of us, and he couldn't put aside that specter.

His anguish was genuine, and he gave a dignity to melancholy.

Another person I miss is Joe Alessi, a father, husband, fellow parishoner and St. Vincent De Paul Society co-worker from St. Anthony's. He died the same week that Mayor Daley did, and at his wake I kept feeling that he was no less in stature than his Honor to those with whom he had contact, but leading a less visible life, of course, than the Mayor, the import of his existence outside of his family might be extinguished with him.

Joe was a teacher, if your mind was open to being taught.

"Listen kid," he'd counsel me on how to work card players at a Smoker to buy Chances; "- have these raffles every half hour-" And he stopped, seeing I was reluctant to dun the guys too much.

"Well, it's just a suggestion," and Joe would shrug-his way of sensing resistance to an idea of his, but then he taught me the lesson of compromise. "If that's too often, why not try selling Split the Deck and-" he'd outline some other tactic.

Joe's life taught him not to get mad when you didn't agree with him; that settling for part of your input was successful too, and to work hard for a good cause no matter whose idea it was or who led it.

My contact with him was brief compared to his sharing with his family or those who worked with him for years, but his effect on me was just as longlasting.

Alright, I'll leave them all "sleeping on the hill ," as Edgar Lee Masters the Illinois Poet would say.

But as Dave Etter another Illinois poet wrote in his poem,

"The Forgotten Graveyard":

I have left my townsmen down below
under the shadows of Town Hall:
religious fakers, Republicans,
the windbags at the barber shop

On this hill, the clean smell of skunk.
The ape-faced trees crouch like gnarled boot-
blacks
over the yellow tombstones;
and there is a bird's nest—a torn blue wig.

But I am at home among the dead,
the deformed, the discolored.
A woodpecker joyfully carves his hole.
The sunset sweetens the mouth of a leaf.

It's nice to get away from the superficiali-
ties that surround us. But don't be afraid to let
your thoughts at times go to those who've left us:
if they come to mind, they must be deserving.

The dead don't have to have an unhealthy
control of our lives; understood, it can be the
simple honesty I've always liked in reading another of Etter's poems,

"Sunday in Kankakee County:

Water from the pump,
a rusty trowel:
red-geraniums
are well planted
now on both sides
of your gravestone

The prairie wind,
the leaves of grass,
the forest smell
of these cedar trees:
Oh how I wish I had come sooner.

Please forgive me.
Here, let me wash
that birdcrap off
your middle name.
There, that's better.
Louise I love you.

By John Aranza 13

YOUR SHOPPING LIST - CRAFTERS AND ARTISTS ON THE STREET:

#	Name	Item
#1001-A	SUSAN J. THORNTON	Drawings & Paintings
#1001-B	PATRICIA J. LASSAND	Oil Paintings
#1001-C	MARY C. RAUHUT	Water Color Paints
#3113	CHRISTENSEN'S OLDE POP CORN WAGON	
#3114	JIM LUKAS	Photography
##116	REBEKAH FELDMAN	Painting & Portraits
#3317	LULA JORDAN & LLYOD ADAMS	Handcrafted Stained Glass Candle Holders and Mirror Wall Plaques
#3118	ROBERT GILBERT	Hand Made Wooden Toys
#3134	MARGARET GRGEK	Chocolates Novelties Made Out of Chocolates
#3138	VIRGINIA M. ZABA	Wood/Plaster/Neddle-Craft and Crochet Items
#3139-A	CHRIS & DEBBIE SCHREIMER	The Art of Investing Your Money
#3139-B	Dr. Clyman	Advice on "Staying Healthy."
#3140	EDITH M. PIETRZYK	Ceramic items and Neddlework
#3200S	VIDA KANAPECKAS (GABALA)	Stained Glass and Ethnic Printed T-Shirts
#3214AL	JEAN DAVIS	Woodcraft
#3216	PAT KELLEY	Ceramics
#VFW-3217	DIANE MYRON	Pickle on a Stick Food
#3300	JOHN SANTIAGO	Hot Dogs
#3213	IRENE HERNDON	Crochet items

CHICAGO AREA SEA SCOUTS
MORGAN STREET COUNCIL BOOTH OF PASTERIES
MORGAN STREET COUNCIL INFORMATION BOOTH

The Bridgeport/South Morgan Street "EXPO" is a non-for-profit organization dedicated to encouraging and providing art and craft activities in the Bridgeport Area.

Welcome to the Second MORGAN/BRIDGEPORT -- "EXPO" and STREET FESTIVAL organized by the Bridgeport/Morgan Street Council, and presented Sunday, Sept 9th, 1984. 10:00A.M. until 7:00 P.M. Come out and enjoy music, ethnic food, ethnic shopping, see and hear performances and shop at the many craft & artist displays.

BOARD OF DIRECTORS of the BRIDGEPORT'S SOU MORGAN STREET COUNCI

CHAIRWOMEN:
Inge Raha
PRESIDENT:
Ruth DePeder
VICE-PRESIDENT:
Harriet Labouskas
TREASURER:
Kenneth Rutkowski, Sr
SECRETARY:
Dolores Rutkowski

EXPO-COORDINATOR:
Marie T. Bazner
PLANNER:
Dolores and Kenneth Rutkowski.
STREET & BUSINESS PLANNER:
Inge Raha

SUNDAY, SEPTEMBER 9, 1984

THE OPENING CEREMONY OF THE SECOND ANNUAL BRIDGE-PORT/SOUTH MORGAN STREET ART "EXPO" AND STREET FESTIVAL WILL BE AT 31st STREET AT 11:00 A.M.

Ribbon cutting ceremonies we will be honored with the presence of States Attoreny Richard Daley, Alderman Patrick M. Huels; District Commander Tim Daly; Ward Committeeman John Daley; Inge Raha, Chairwomen of the Morgan Street Council; Ruth DePeder, President of the Morgan Street Council Dolores and Ken Rutkowski, Planners of "EXPO 84," Marie T. Bazner, Coordinator of "EXPO 84," John Aranza, Master of Ceremonies; Patrick Finley; The Boy Scouts of America; American Legion Flanders Post; Knights of Columbus and the DeLaSalle Marching Band.

FOR YOUR ENTERTAINMENT:

33rd Street: 11-11:30 A.M. States Attoreny Law Mobile.

12:00 Noon - The Mounted Police

Crafters and artists and food vendors will dot both sides of the streets from 33rd Street to 31st Street

32nd Street: SOUTH STAGE (POORMEN'S PUB)

10:00 A.M. unitl 1:00 KoKo a professional clown will paint faces and give rides on her Magic Scooter.

1:30 P.M. KoKo will give a Puppet Show for the children.

3P.M.-7 P.M. The Polka Sensations will entertain and there will be a "POLKA CONTEST" 1st, 2nd and 3rd prizes will be awarded.

31st Street: NORTH STAGE Joe Hudson (CORNER TAVERN)

3-4 P.M. LECHICI DANCERS of the Polish Youth Assoc.

5-7 P.M. BREAK-DANCES CONTEST (2 - $50.00 BONDS) Prize for groups: 10-11-12 & group 13-14-15

Places to eat: at POORMEN'S PUB
BRIDGEPORT QUALITY MARKET
LINA'S PIZZA
MRS. KELLY'S STORE STAND
Joe & Dwyane Hudson (Corner Tavern)

ARCHITECTURAL AND HISTORICAL TOURS WILL BE AT: 1:00 P.M. also at 2:00 P.M. and the last one at 3:00 P.M. The tours will be conducted by John Aranza, Professor William Burns and Richard Schultz.

* * * * * * * * * * * * * *

We wish to thank the following businesses for material gifts we received for "EXPO 84."

LEFTON'S CHINA
WIDMANS HARDWARE
HELEN'S CARD SHOP

A "Special Thank You" to the MAYOR'S OFFICE OF SPECIAL EVENTS" and SPIEGEL, INC. for their donations.

WE're proud of our following donors:

Edwards Heating & Cooling Company
Tony Garcia

Timothy Degnan Campaign Committee
Nick & Ruth DePeder
Joe Harris Hardware Company
Inge Raha
Jean and Rita Sunsak
Bridgeport News

Morgan Paint
T. Fisher and C. Boravina
Bill Byrne
Charles Govern
Lee and Jennie Holland
Anthony Pusateri
Bernie Wolf & Jeff Rohrsen
Bridgeport Pharmacy

SPECIAL THANKS TO COM. TIM DALY AND SGT. JOSEPH SEPULVEDA OF THE 9th DISTRICT POLICE FOR THEIR ADVICE AND HELP. ALS TO THE DEPARTMENT OF STREETS AND SANITATION FOR THEIR VER EFFICIENT RESPONSE TO THE "EXPO" NEEDS. ALSO "THANK YOU" T RAY KUJAWA.

Brochure for the Morgan street art fair cir 1984

The Morgan Street Art Fair

The first Morgan St. Multi-Media Expo (Art Fair) is over, but I hope it just begun.

Will there be others? Will its aesthetic expressions be reflected in future Morgan St. life? Or will the program pamphlets we carried home be our only reminder of the thousands of people that walked slowly and happily through that cultural bazaar?

It was a pleasantly warm enough Sunday in the upper 70's, and Morgan was cleared curb-to-curb from 31st to 34th, barricades erected stopping all traffic and not one car was on the street.

A special mood was there; a proud feeling for that neighborhood. Like a parent for its children playing the piano. And its children were our own, displaying their creations. Look. See. Jonas the sign painter from 34th and Halsted whose wider range of talent was reflected in his realistic and impressionistic paintings.

One of us, Mary Rauhut, from 31st and Union, recent graduate of Northern Illinois University with her pastel watercolor prints. Beverly De Pass and a variety of caricatures, editorial drawings and sketches. A waitress from the Hickory Pit and a student from De La Salle High School.

If you've ever been in the old St. Patrick Day Parades down State Street or walked the neighborhood streets in '67 when the Great Blizzard made high ridges of them, you know the different perspective you get of the buildings on either side of you from the middle of the street.

On Richard Schultz's marvelous Official Walking Tours, you sensed the heritage once more of the Poles and Lithuanians whose distinctive buildings of glazed tiles, ornamental facades and unique bays and cupolas have been somewhat silent and overlooked.

Forgotten, as time sometimes forgets, that is the area of the first Lithuanian Parish in Chicago (St. George's); of the first consecrated Polish Church in Chicago (St. Mary's of Perpetual Help); of the first female undertaker in the State of Illinois; of the child-hood home of Bobo Rockefeller; or of the little neighborhood bakery that became the Holsum Bread company.

That was then, but the Morgan Street Council with this Fair successfully showed us what we could be now: artists in those unused storefronts; musicians playing again in the Ballroom; new businesses, perhaps, such as the stained glass, knitting and jewelry crafts that we saw. And it will take that cooperative effort that also had Committeeman Daley, Alderman Huels, 9th Police District Commander Roger Whalen and our resident 15th District Commander Timothy Daly and his attractive family there, too.

--But there are other alternatives.

Pictured at the ribbon cutting ceremony that began the Morgan St. Fair are l to r: Patrick Finley, treasurer Valentine's Boys club; John Daley, Democratice Ward Committeeman; Inge Raha, chairperson Morgan Street Council; Patrick Huels, alderman of the 11th ward; Roger Whalen, Commander of Chgo. Police Dept. 9th District, and John Aranza, area resident, realtor, historian, and writer for the Bridgeport News.

One of the recent businesses to open on Morgan is licensed for one purpose, but it also has four or five video games in front and one or more pool tables in the back. Isn't there more to us than that?

A young woman asked while on the architectural tour: "You seem to have so much going unrecorded and unprotected here in your neighborhood. Is there anything being done about it?"

Maybe you should answer. Is there?

By John Aranza 15

You're Right - It's Wrong

Wrong Street, that is. Twenty-ninth used to be Stearns, named after the owners of the quarry, but it was also called Wrong Street. (From Stewart to Wentworth, it was Swift Place.) Now that you know your Wrong, a brief genealogy about some other tantalizing neighborhood street names.

Being a developer guaranteed the distinction of having a thoroughfare named after you, though how long does that fame last? In Brighton Park, Francisco was formerly Underwood, a developer there. Remember? (But another, Kedzie's name, still remains.)

Canaryville's 43rd Place was Gordon and 45th Place was Baker, developers too. Bridgeport's Throop was Fox (and once our only Main Street) ; 32nd Place, Springer; and now only Halsted's memory endures, a Philadelphia banker and investor-friend of Chicago's first Mayor, Wiliam B. Ogden, whose asphalt testimony is elsewhere.

Shurtleff has been forgotten in Armour Square; his street was changed to Fifth Avenue, copying New York's, then to its present Wells Street for Captain William Wells, killed in the Fort Dearborn Massacre of 1812. I'm sure the people on Lloyd are grateful to their developer, but probably just as glad it's no longer called Fake Street.

Giving Christian names. to streets was as common in the 1800's as it is in a new subdivision today. What's left of Mary Street is north of Archer and the Stevenson Expressway, an unmarked corridor east of Stark. What at different times was Heldmaier, Cologne or Water, is now Eleanor Street; Parnell was once William Street in Canaryville only; and 31st Place west of Morgan was James; and 32nd treet, Elmira.

If you could afford a home on both streets, you could move between seasons from Union to Lowe Avenue—originally Winter and Summer Streets.

Far away places? Canal Street was Hanover, named after the German city; then commemorating the Illinois and Michigan Canal. Twenty-third Street was Palo Alto, and 24th Street was Monterey. Emerald was named to symbolize Ireland, the Emerald Isle. And if you feel yourself wanting to hum "Hail to the Chief" while on 30th Street, east of Stewart, it's because it was first named Whitehouse Place.

Famous people (besides yourselves)? Wentworth was named after twice Chicago Mayor of the 1850's and 60's, the 6'6" tall "Long" John Wentworth. Twenty-second Place was Chopin: 25th Place, Kossuth, after the Hungarian statesman; 28th Pl., Napoleon: Shields was Garibaldi, after the Italian patriot; Parnell, the Irish nationalist; and 35th Street, Douglas Avenue, after the Senator, developer and "Little Giant" of the Lincoln-Douglas debates, Stephen A. Douglas, whose tomb you can visit at 35th and Lake Park.

Thirty-fifth to Thirty-eighth Place, between Halsted and Morgan, were once A, B, C, D, E and F Streets. And if you met someone at Onondago and Laurel, you would be at 34th and Morgan-one an Indian name, the other named after the branches the Greeks used to make wreaths for victors; hence, signifying honor: Honorable Morgan Street.

Auburn was also Tucker before it was changed to Lituanica, the name of the heroic Darius and Girenas' airplane. Hoey near Archer and Poplar is shorter than Short Street. And Loomis was Deering, its name following the police station incorporated in 1871 at Archer and Deering to 35th and Lowe.

And you can easily learn more about our neighborhoods at the Chicago Public Library, the Municipal Reference Library or the Chicago Historical Society. Go. Discover. Enjoy!

-All of this just made me think of how I used to go to the show at Ridgely and Summer Streets and see Norma Jean Baker and Bernie Schwartz. Oh, Wow. See ya's.

John Aranza

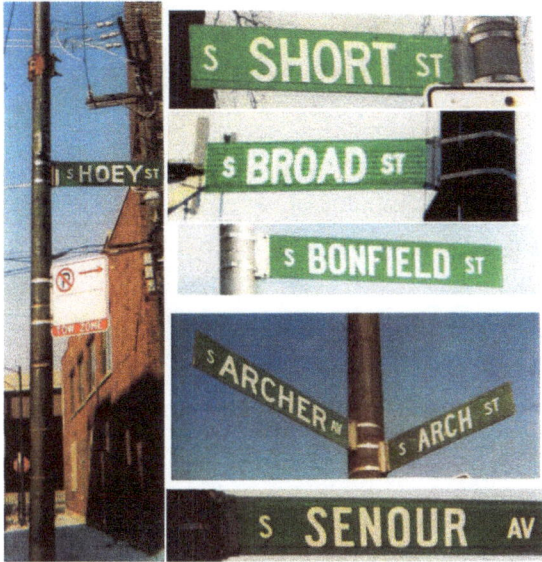

Hoey, at less than 150', is one of Chicago's shortest streets! Short and Broad streets are not named for their size as you might think but developers. The Corner of Archer Avenue and Arch Street. Don't get confused! Bonfield St a Neighborhood Chicago Police Commander whose name will be forever associated with the 1886 Haymarket Affair. Senour Avenue named after a one-time resident paint company.

Mea Culpa

I didn't want to go to Mass last Sunday again. Maybe it's because I have to go (for my son's approval or for fear of eternal damnation if I don't). Maybe it's because of the futility I feel in saying I'm sorry and sinning again. Or maybe it's because I can never find the philosophical quiet of my youth—when you could find an open church when you needed one, and sitting there in silence, you knew you were communicating with You Know Who.

But I go. And Boze always does something to break my stride like skaters used to get bumped in the Roller Derby, as if slipping on ice and losing their balance and falling backwards to let me know why I'm supposed to be there.

Lately it's been through the marvelously insightful sermons of St. Jerome's pastor, Father Kucan. God speaks through that man. His simple truths become so powerful; he is swept along in saying them. Sunday, he talked about an apostle's belief that was similar to a phrase by Thoreau I wish I could follow: that a man in rich in proportion to the things he could afford to leave behind. It was as if God said Aranza, that's for being like Thomas and questioning the relevancy of your religion.

As much as I was pleased in doing it, I regarded visiting churches on Holy Thursday as a bit routine-oriented. So what happened? At Lucia's Church, I met Rosa Fratto, whose friendship I shouldn't have let several years intervene.

Every woman isn't the Blessed Mother, but surely every mother is blessed. And Rosa is the precious ointment of her family. That night she was bringing a meal to share with the other parishioners at a Holy Thursday dinner.

"John, why you no come see us anymore?" Her eyes were tired-looking, but caring and beautiful like a Jonathan David sculpture. There was no valid reason for not. Lady Madonna, I thought of the Beatles' song. Saintly. Humble. Elegant.

My wife, son, and I stopped in her kitchen (isn't that the soul of an Italian mother's home?) after Easter Sunday Mass. Rosa was preparing sauces for the afternoon dinner, and Maria, her last child at home, stood attentively nearby.

When her husband Nandino came up from the basement, it was suddenly a bonanza of wine and bread

A pre-teen when this article was written, Maria Frattto Sheppard now, stands in front of her own Italian cookie store, Biscotti's Galore and More with her mother Rosa on the corner of 32nd and S. Wells Sreet, down the block from her childhood home. Maria learned her skills in her mother's kitchen, and with her help and her husband's family created this neighborhood continuum.

By John Aranza 17

with cheese and sausage in it to take home, and coffee and whiskey and cake there.

Who wouldn't cry? How do you laugh through your tears and explain to your nine year old that you're really happy? How much more admiration can you feel for a person, when her husband tells you that she went back to work only 2 weeks after a back operation after working full-time for twenty years?

Well, the Sun-Times' calls have been unreturned by me this past week, by a reporter trying to gather material for still another story on Bridgeport. I'm being selfish, but it's like being stripped of the little secrets we hold store in our hearts when anyone tries to focus on the deeply-felt experiences we've accumulated from our lives in Bridgeport.

And yet, I'll probably make that call: I've been given some exquisite moments, undeservedly, for just going through the motions. And the rest of Chicago should know about all of you Rosa's out there, and all of the other fascinations we seem to offer.

Something Was Moving Out There

How many of you secretly are glad that another season of the church, Easter, is over? For the attention it got? The Time it demanded for masses and devotions? The uneasiness we may have felt thinking on our wrong doings? (Or do you simply prefer the 'smack-em in the eye real good' of the "Thorn Birds" for all religions?)

On Holy Thursday, I went to evening mass at St. Jerome's and then I visited the neighborhood churches, but I made so many re-discoveries I was ashamed of myself for routinely feeling that I just 'had to go' to begin with.

I always sensed a medieval presence, a centuries-old expression in the cavernous awe of St. Gabriels. Basilica; splendor, ornate, I felt, in St. Mary's and St. Barbara's. I understand, I think, the theory for simple altar tables and unadorned modern churches-St. John Nepomucene illustrates that within its old building-trying not to focus on images or statuary, but instead of considering them distractions, I viewed those other churches as grandiloquent designs reflecting the

Entrance of St. Anthony De Padua church. 28th Place and S. Wallace. Mosaic designed by Professor Theodor Rauecker the Royal Bavarian Mosaic Art Est. ,Munich-Solln, Germany. (1914)

same fervor of those parishioners.

At St. George's, my son whispered about the Gothic architecture which he couldn't define that impressed him as he pointed interestedly at the spires of the wooden altars repeated at the ends of all the pews. The spiney-looking branches decorating one side of the altar were simple, humble, folk-art expressions of the Lithuanian culture.

At Santa Lucia Church, I looked with childish curiosity again at the statues of St. Cecelia and St. Agnes, laying as if in glass-fronted crypts beneath the side altars. At St. Anthony's Church the following evening, I accompanied my mother to Good Friday services. And Dr. Frank Pellegrini and the adult choir sounded like members of a cloister, as if no one heard, only God, but representing all of us there, as they fervently sang out the Stabat Mater and other sorrowful hymns in soft, undulating cadence.

And the entire weekend, I thought of the excellence in us that faith inspired. Not unmanly or false or pretentious or showy. And not creating feelings like the overly-stressed commercial aspects of Christmas, that once we flashed the last neon smile for some unwanted gift, we were glad it was behind us.

The visiting people criss-crossing each other from their parishes were as open as those churches. And the art, talent and creativity of each neighborhood revealed itself in those decorations, choirs and services.

Something was out there among us, I thought. Something. An other-worldly feeling, real or imagined, accented by the hushed movements of those people even outside of the churches.

Homecoming

My nephew John Condic's wife, Lena, called me that a co-worker's aunt was making a special return to Bridgeport.

So Saturday morning, Gertrude Scanlon Polaskey made her first thorough visit to the neighborhood in 62 years; leaving here in 1914, and then moving to Grand Rapids, Michigan with her husband for his job in 1922.

I met this 86 year old 'archaelogist' with brown and white hair, with her nephew Robert Klaus and his wife Joan and their children, across from St. Bridget's where her parents were married at the original church in 1882. She reminded me of the genteel-looking actress Helen Hayes, enunciating clearly in a glass-ringing voice and with equally lucid recall.

Although our destination was her birthplace at 2972 South Loomis, the walking tour getting there was the greater pleasure, just as the anticipation and fantasizing of planning a trip is sometimes better than taking it.

" - Lemmer's Tailor Shop was there," she pointed to a boarded-up storefront in the vacant four-story building at 2918 S. Archer, identifying the dead, breathing life into the lifeless where we walk familiar streets with unfamiliar pasts always wondering "who we were before we became what we are?"

"And Mrs. O'Sullivan had a candy store there too. The pastor hinted we should spend our pennies at her shop as she was a parishioner."

Walking to Kunka's Pharmacy, at the corner of Archer and Loomis, was going to Charley Baker's to her. Inside, the present owner Henry Greifenstein, gave her an old label proving it was a bakery started in 1860 in the first building on that site and named after Charley Baker until he died in the 1920's.

I've never seen anything bring more pride out of people than their being able to exactly recall the past, as if they were bearers of a sacred trust; and much more commanding having lived it, as she.

She asked the half-her-age Henry about a Niersbach family, who ran a dairy from the rear of their home on the block. He answered proudly, like quoting from the Book of Genesis, knowing he was identifying Roots too, that the daughter, now perhaps in her eighties still came to the drug store.

And that feeling of somehow owning the past, that can only be understood and shared by those who lived it or carefully keep its memory, continued.

By John Aranza 19

We had a conversation with Gertrude Finucane whose door we knocked at on South Loomis, explaining Scanlon's journey back to her neighborhood womb, and learning that the Finucane family owned and lived in this building for over 100 years.

As Scanlon determined Mrs. Finucane was thirty years or so younger than herself, and said she knew her husband's father, Bill Finucane, she created this image to me of a female Methuselah in a print dress. They spoke reverently of long-ago families, of Consodines, O'Mearas and Reeds, as if they were the closest of friends, though they never met before.

And we all laughed as they reminisced about a Doctor Crowley when they said "he never gave kids any ether, and you could hear them screaming down on the street from his dental office in Kunka's building, scared out of their wits."

She introduced herself to Ron and Mary Mc Nicholas on Loomis, in their forties, whose children are the fifth generation of that family in their home. She explained that she knew his grandparents, and that her sister, the chauffeuring nephew's mother, was born next door.

It didn't matter that her family two-flat at 2972 Loomis was demolished years ago and that she discovered a new bungalow in its place-Gertrude knew what was beyond grief - because her memories were a stunning reality of children's children living on the block, "maybe in modernized buildings" she observed, but continuing for her what was her early life.

She recognized a Marion and Dolores Davidson on Loomis "—you're Jessie Grady's daughters, aren't you? who married John Davidson?"

They were reunited instantly recalling common memories, smiling that Gertrude's family lived next door for a while and how a patrolman Stanley, who lived there too, called his son home each night blowing his whistle.

Our last visit was to Mary and Deliah Kane's on South Bonaparte; strangers to her but then immediate confidants in what they held within them. "Remember Mrs. Reed who handed out the bathing suits at Mark White Square (McGuane Park) pool, maybe 10

sizes too big? You had to take what was given to you, but you had to get out soon for the next group coming in anyway."

As I listened to and watched the three of them, graceful, elegant statespersons to scenarios unseen and scripts unheard, I knew I was witness to a partial glimpse into respectable yet exciting lives formed in a more innocent time as their past seemed to me. Affirmed by their wholesomeness, I only wished I could capture and recapture the essence of them forever, walking in and out of the happiness of their recollections through doors closed to us now called yesterday, which always seemed to hold that fascination which makes us want to know what was on those other sides, it we could only enter.

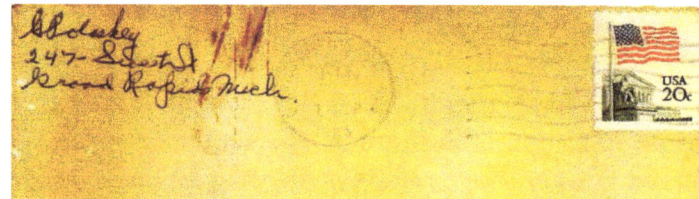

Hey Mister, Want Yer Shoes Shined?

The summer-like days last week spawned warm-weather activities in young people, as suddenly bursted upon us as unnoticed buds that were blooming.

Who can explain how flies and ants were instantaneously in the house when the temperature unexpectedly reached the seventies, as neighborhood children' outside were roller skating, playing softball in the streets, and already in money-making activities?

I already had seen two lemonade stands with the usual eager but somewhat fearful-of-failing look of eight year old owners, "- who'll probably drink up their profits," my wife remarked.

It reminded me of my youthful attempt at making mad-money. My father didn't think too much of selling watermelons off a horse and wagon I was going to rent at 43rd and Emerald, but young people only consider what's adventuresome.

Eventually it was the "Teen Cleaners." I thought of that name and activity to sum up everything me and my friends figured we were capable of doing: cleaning out attics and basements, mowing lawns, washing and painting. I can't even remember all of the things I claimed us miracle men could do in the 5,000 handbills we had printed and distributed.

Well, we got our first job. It was to paint the back room and toilet area of Frank Suchy's barber shop that was next to the Modern Pharmacy on 31st Street. Barry McMeel and I took this on, while Joe Casale and Billy Notidas had an assignment in Oak Lawn. Sure, we had a Suburban branch. (The wind must have carried our circulars that far.)

We were nervous starting our first job, and young people will always be afraid of upsetting adults, won't they? And we did.

Suchy was thin like John Carradine or Oscar Levant, and he could do a slow burn like Edgar Kennedy. And he did.

Barry and I were probably painting the first walls of our lives, and Frank came back to see how we were doing.

"What's this'?" we helped raise his blood pressure. We looked at the walls, each other, and then the brushes, just as he did.

What could be wrong? Barry and I thought together, but were afraid to ask.

Frank grabbed my brush and wanted to know if I knew what it was for.

"I got it out of our shed at home," I tried to explain knowingly.

"This ain't for painting," he said. It was either a white-wash or a wallpaper paste brush, and the paint on the walls did look as if it were put on with a rake- like the channel rows of a freshly planted farm field- alternating paint and the old wall.

That's all I can recall of that job.

Joe and Billy lost theirs too. We only got bits and pieces about an owner's teenage daughter and flirting going on and a bucket of soapy water being spilled on oak hardwood floors .

And then there was no more "Teen Cleaners." I wonder why?

But there's 4,998 circulars out there somewhere testifying to our youth, and if we only were handed a paint brush, as we were, after we were married, we'd intuitively know what to do with one and certainly would have been more successful.

Ah Barry, Frank, folks-we were just ahead of our time.

Ahead of our time.

By John Aranza 21

This Hammer's For Hire

Previously I wrote how I failed as a Teen Cleaner, but that was before my time had arrived.

It wasn't until I managed the building at 3155-59 S. Wallace that I became ingenious at property maintenance.

F & M TV and John Shultz rented the stores on the first floor, and there were eight four-room apartments on the 2nd & 3rd floors.

In one of those flats, two deaf mutes lived. (You could learn from them how to deal with life & adjust, such as the series of lights they connected that flashed inside when you pushed a door bell button.)

Well, my real estate classes stressed that a building manager obtains maximum net income by proficient techniques, but it usually came down to who you paid what to get repairs done.

When they left me a note saying that water leaked down from the kitchen above into their pantry, I tried the best way to save owner Ed Weiss money that I could think of: "Why not make the repairs myself?"

I explained to the tenants that I was going to make the patch, and thinking back on it, their look was either that they didn't understand my clumsy sign language like a tourist in a foreign country, or they were incredulous that I was going to attempt it.

I returned with a ladder and tools, and confidently I smashed at the plaster to clean out the loosened area. But by hitting upward, I broke the wood laths between the joists.

I tried filling the square foot area with plaster, but it wouldn't hold to the laths that were angled up into the ceiling. If only I could get them down even with the rest of the ceiling, I thought, the patch would hold.

I figured that something heavy, tied to those laths would pull them down, and then I could complete my work.

The only thing handy was my hammer. I looped a string around the laths and tied it to the hammer, so it hung a few feet below the ceiling. It kept the laths pulled down, and I made the patch.

When they came to see what I had done, I triumphantly let them read my lips and interpret my motions why a hammer was hanging by a string out of the center of their pantry ceiling.

They looked up curiously, but I explained with a snipping movement with my fingers that I would return the next day to cut the weight down and fill the hole where the string was.

When it was over, I was glad that no one else had seen what I had done. I knew I had taken advantage of their disability, but I kept pantomiming that what I was doing was customary. But that was 20 years ago. Like I said, I might have failed as a Teen Cleaner, only to triumph later on.

Rrrrring. It's my telephone. Excuse me a moment.

"Yes Bob?" (It's my brother-in-law.)

"-you need me to take a rare antique beveled glass out while you plane your front door? Sure I'll help you."

(I'll talk to you again soon. I have to go now. But really, it feels good when you know you can help someone.)

"-yeah Bob, I'll get my hammer and I'll be right over,"

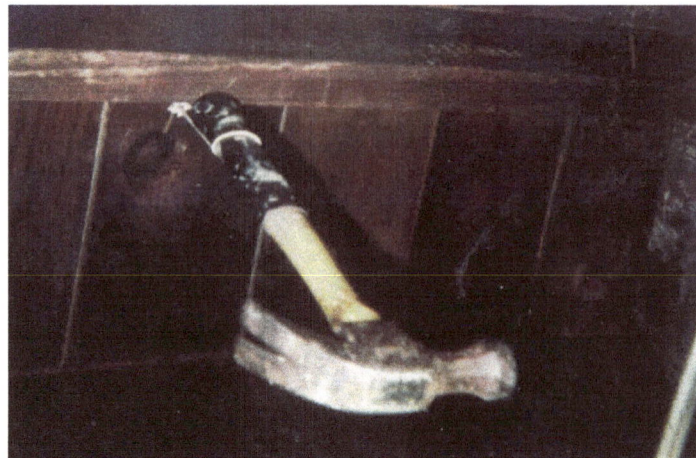

The Boys for All Reasons

New Year's Eve child and Father Time drawings
Art by Beverly De Pass

In a way, I felt sorry for those men who spent $2,200.00 last month to have their dream-fantasys fulfilled in Arizona: A week with the '69 Cubs at a mock Spring Training camp. Oh they had their close-ups with Randy Hundley and Jim Hickman, but many also paid with painfully little-used muscles.

Here in the neighborhood, I thought, some of us have never stopped doing in sports what we've always been able to do-in McGuane Park's Over 30 Basketball League now.

The team that I'm a small part of is Ted's MBA. Jim Marzano is 47, Bruce Alphin 46 and Bill Green a much one day older than me at 43. Jack Keeler is 41, and Ken Kolerich 41, and his only complaint in the tournament so far was before our first game when he protested having to be a "skin" (we didn't have our jerseys yet); and when he took his shirt off, we all could see why he was resisting. All right-I'll say it. You're forcing me to talk about a friend; Ken is not thin. And yes, next to him Chris Balich is Adonis. But like Babe Ruth, Kenny's bulk (as Spencer Tracy referred to his own "adult" size) doesn't interfere with his superior skills. Tom Balich at 32 thinks that and plays like he should be a Chicago Bull, and with Bob Green 30 and Ed Walz 40 and his faithful companion Greg Danz 37, we're doing quite well. And that's not lording over a turtle race as you might be fooled into thinking by our ages.

The well-known Levato brothers also have a team entered. When I hear their wives and children in the bleachers each Sunday afternoon urging on their gladiators, I think of the song "We Are Family." Jimbo is in his late forties, and his brother Carm is very competative in his early fifties. Do they what? -Oh yes, they still engage in the lively art of conversation with the Refs. And the entire team is fiercely loyal and protective of each other like tag-team wrestlers. (I'll be right back-I hope. That's them at my door wanting to see me about something.)

On McCarthy's, Fausto Manzera at 54 is the typical Boy for All Reasons-a successful Harold Stassen in neighborhood softball, football or basketball tournaments. His squared profile is reminiscent of our Presidents on Mt. Rushmore, and I'm sure that all of you have acquaintences like him who give hints of what they were in their other lives or what they could or should be. Fausto, a general, perhaps, revealing something from his Mexican heritage. When he's bringing the ball up court, I can envision medals and bars pinned across his wide, expansive chest and his thick, black moustache and dark surveying eyes further shadowed heroically by a braided military hat-and when he's motioning to his teammates with one hand to move around the baselines, shouting "C'mon, C'mon," he could just as well be Patton or Zapata directing his troops: "Don't stand there. Move-this is war."

If a Most Valuable Actor's Award is to be given after the tournament, I nominate Charley Viskocil who brilliantly performs being fouled by collapsing like a man just shot by firing squad.

But as jokingly as I may try to describe our actions, the tournament does represent more than just what a few players say: "it's only a game. We're not out here to win; I'm here to have a good time."

By John Aranza 23

For many, it's an effortless display of talent. With some of us, its on slower but brave legs "try'n", as Jerry Lee Lewis sings in Middle Age Crazy, "to prove' we still can." Still for others, it's being "macho," or saying no to age or not having aged at all.

But it's also seeking recognition with deft-moves or ball-handling skills in an every-day world that may not always recognize us for everything that we are.

And too, it is that tough, competative feeling that God unexplicably sewed into the fabric of the neighborhood (though I perceive the unyielding human spirit at any sport event). And with that understanding, we can hustle for a ball and bump into each other most times without a fight erupting; and it is in that sense too, with Jimbo and Carm and the rest of their brothers, all of us out there really are family.

You're Not Alone, Sandy

Last week, while I was writing a frivolous article about my friends, a very sad mother's letter appeared nearby my column in the paper telling how her 10 and 3 year-olds were robbed recently.

"Mom, why are there people like that in the world?" her uncomprehending child asked her.
It's not easy for us adults to fathom the injustices of life, so can you imagine the confusion in those children's minds?

At least that mother in her letter showed no despair, some frustration and bitterness, understandably, yes, but I'm sure that she's nurturing her children not to have any recrimination in them.

If F. Scott Fitzgerald wrote in a despairing mood "But at three o'clock in the morning, a forgotten package has the same tragic importance as a death sentence, and the cure doesn't work, and in a real dark night of the soul it is always three o'clock in the morning day after day.", conversely it must be true that at 12:00 noon of every day there's hope in all well-intentioned persons like her. We don't know what caused those other children to hurt hers, but we do know the madness that could result if we all conditioned ourselves and our children to retaliate eventually in kind, thinking: "Wait until I get even."

It's so difficult to determine when pacifism should end and self-defense or retribution should begin, but better Sandy Huss's example. Train your children morally correct, and hope that the rest of creation does too.

There's no guarantee your way will be emulated, but there's always hope that it will be.

If for nothing else, I selfishly at times don't commit wrongs because I say to myself: "I wouldn't want someone to do that to me." That doesn't make me right, I know, but whatever our motivations, we all hope for peace and uninterfered enjoyment in our lives.

So I think that many of us in the neighborhood understand your children's loss, and in supporting and encouraging you, we are doing so for ourselves.

Keep your children's thoughts positive, as we all must try to keep our own.

And if any of you read something humorous that I write while your personal crisis continue, it's not that I or this newspaper is unmindful of the essence of everyday living (ask my Editor, to see the serious articles I propose); but she's right, I can understand better now, when she encourages me: "John, the neighborhood needs the things you write about because it makes them feel good about themselves, and we need that , too."

Life needs you too, Sandy, to keep your family and others uplifted, and I know this newspaper realized that when they published your letter.

How many of us try to be witty, popular, creative, successful and such in life? I know I try to be in my writing, and then something happens with unintentioned poignancy and deserves more recognition than anything else in the world.

I felt your article was that way.
So let me paraphrase Joyce Kilmer's poem:
"...stories are written by
Fools like me,
But only God can
Make a tree."

Yesterday, Once More

I never met Karen Carpenter or attended a performance of hers. If she had a TV special, I didn't see it or guest appearances if she made them. And yet, like Emily Dickenson when she wrote: "I never saw a moor, I never saw the sea; Yet know I how the heather looks, And what a wave must be," I felt an intimacy with her as if I knew every detail of her life. Some of her songs evoked such emotional responses within me, that like all great artists—novelists, singers and actors—you feel that they are speaking for you alone. And when I heard the unexpected news of her death, I couldn't understand why the world didn't pause and hold a collective breath.

Death from anorexia nervosa—something about a fixation with staying thin—the words themselves sounded like a cruel mimicry. If she had died from drug abuses that we've sadly become accustomed to from rock performers, but this—

I first heard of Karen Carpenter when "We've Only Just Begun" was sung at my niece's wedding. I really thought it was bland sounding. Works of art affect each of us differently, but I knew that she was apparently speaking for that generation with flowers in their hair, just as "I Love You Truly" did for those before me.

It wasn't until I heard her sing "Mr. Postman" that I was affected by the range of her art. Unlike some performers aping 50's songs, you felt that she wanted to sing this way out of her love for that style, and she created a unique, almost reverent version of rock-and-roll.

I was sure of this when I heard "It's Yesterday Once More". Not sounding like some singers tiring and making fun of what made them popular, she mellowed wistfully and longingly—or made it seem so—like a torch singer from the 40's when she sung:

"Those where such happy times
And not so long ago—
How I wondered where they'd gone,
But they're back again
Like a long lost friend,
All the songs I loved so well

Every Sha-la-lalah
Every Woe-oh-oh
Still shines
Every Shing-a-ling-a-ling
That they're starling to sing,
So fine."

(And then a classical sound was heard like the Beatles introduced into rock songs in "Eleanor Rigby") and then—

"All my best memories
Come back clearly to me—
Some can even make me cry,
Just like before:
It's yesterday once more."

When I heard her sing "Superstar" and its provocative "Long ago, and oh so far away, I fell in love with you, before the second show," and the not-childish sounding chorus consoling "Babe-ee, Baby, Baby, Baby, Bay-ay-ay-bee, I luh-uh-uv you" –she romanticized the commonplace into seldom-expressed sensitive moods.

I hope that no up-coming story—anywhere, at any time—ever tries to headline: "The Real Karen Carpenter." For me, through the miracle of recordings, I think I know what she really was like. But that's the way I am. And if through another miracle she can read this wherever she is Thanks, from one of the nameless millions you reached out to, Superstar.

P.S. When I commented to my high-school friend Wally Chodor that I wanted to write about Karen Carpenter, he said: "John, you're too serious. Life's too short to be like that. Live for the day."

Well, what could I say. I couldn't begin to explain that was only one side of me. Then last week,

By John Aranza 25

I took Elaine and our nine-year-old son for a ride. We stopped at a red light somewhere on Archer, and I hunched over the steering wheel and I grabbed the shift and started sounding out: "Vroom, Vroom," as if I were revving the engine like I did when I was a teenager out riding with my boy friends. Johnny Boy was laughing at this, but I told him:

"Ah, Daddy's not goofy anymore, Son. He's mellowed. I used to really fool around."

"Oh no, Daddy," he said innocently, "—don't feel bad. I think you're still goofy."

So listen, Wally. I want you to know that my son isn't a liar, and you better believe what he says. But don't tell anyone else.

"You're On, Mr. Kohlmann"

Every time I see the movie, "The Best Years of Our Lives", I exhilarate over Hollywood's eloquent dramatizations of the common man. "The Invaders of the Lost Ark" and James Bond are needed entertainment, but how often are we the people portrayed up there as in "The Graduate," or "It's a Wonderful Life," or "An Unmarried Woman," where the plot doesn't seem fictional at all, but the conflict reminds us so much of our everyday lives that we believe the action is real?

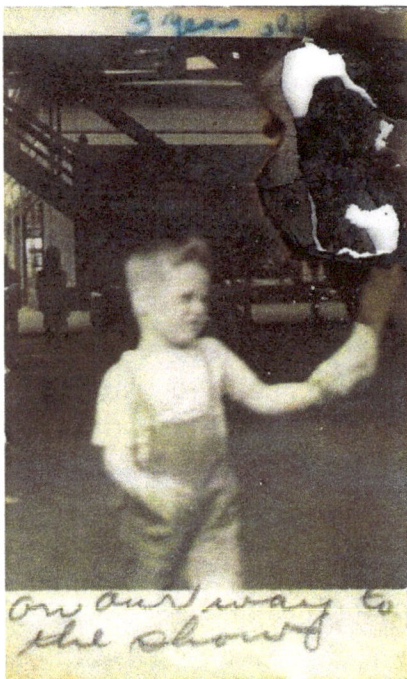

on our way to the show

I can still remember holding my mother's protective hand and seeing the marquee of the State and Lake or the Chicago Theatre blinking around something about "Ten Academy Award Nominations' one late 1940's Downtown.

"The Best Years of Our Lives"—

And how fantastic, I thought, when I finally saw the picture on television 20 years or so later. It was a strange connection to my past: an interpretation of another world so

much changed we can hardly believe it ever really existed (Frederic March and Dana Andrews adjusting to civilian life after World War II), and yet it reminded me so much of us, the neighborhood, to me.

We have so few tangible reminders left of that era. Where are those memorials that were on every corner? Flag poles and plaques with the names of those from that block in service; and maybe room for flowers and a concrete star at the base. (I had to pass 31st and Normal to be

sure that one wasn't in the parkway anymore. Did Mickey and Danny Sheehan, Marie and Jimmy Brush, and Little

Eddy and, ghosts, childhood ghosts, all of us, did we really play hide-and-go-seek leaning against that pole?)

I asked Johnny Kohlmann (was I insane pressing him so?) after Mass last Sunday:

"Weren't you something like that? (Thinking of Dana Andrews in the movie returning to a drug store clerk's job, one of us, after being a gunner on a flying fortress.) Didn't you tell me once, John, that you were on bombing missions in the Second World War?"

(I mean what could he think as we sat near the front

room window of his two-flat at 2941 South Wallace: Aranza's asking me about the war, and it's been over almost 40 years. And yet me thinking—Kohlmann—you, me, another neighbor, Jim Johnson, who walked by on the sidewalk outside with his two daughters and his father, their watchful grandfather. You see, we're part of this scenario that's so evocative; so ongoing: that means so much.)

"Johnny," he told me, "I was a waist gunner armorer on a B24."

"Did you sign up for that?" I asked our modest neighbor..

"Sign up?" he laughed and waved his hand at me: "—I was drafted by the Army exactly one year after Pearl Harbor, and I just did what they told me. I was about 30, but after I took an aptitude test at Fort Sheridan, they assigned me to the Air Force."

"Did you want to fly?"
"I was afraid of flying: and I never flew before that."
And yet he became a gunner shooting a machine gun out of an open side bay window of a B24, flying 50 missions over railyards in Yugoslavia, and Northern Italy, the Monte Cassino Abbey, Southern France, Rumania, Austria, Bulgaria, and Czechoslovakia.

"If you didn't wear your protective clothing," he continued, "you'd freeze because it was 20 below zero up there at 25,000 feet. The only thing you could recognize below were farms, like patches, and mountains, and rivers. But when we were attacked by fighter planes, you forget you were alive and you just fought for your life and kept on shooting, watching the tracers guiding your aim."

I thought of Dana Andrews again, perhaps in one of Hollywood's most memorable scenes: sitting in a gunner's bubble of a scrapped B24 he came across in a construction yard while out searching for a job; and he relived the tremor of the war, unable to find peace in Peace.

"Were there celebrations when you came home, John?"

He laughed. Not bitterly but as resignedly as he must have been then: "There were no celebrations; no free meals; no drinks. You were just another civilian returning home. You were glad the war was over, and everything was just like before I left. I went back to work at the Bindery I was at a week after I was discharged."

Dana Andrews selling lotions; Johnny Kohlmann a printer again (now deservedly retired).

And so much like all of the neighborhood, I thought. Doing what has to be done; unceremoniously; asking no favors, an everyday Bridgeport life; yet the steel in our cannons, and the hero of a winning movie unknowingly played before the world with how many more of you out there in common yet heroic featured roles?

''November 22, 1963 12:30 P.M.''

"-we interupt this program for the following special report: 'An attempt has been made on the life of President John F . Kennedv. He and Texas Governor John Connally were shot -while motorcading through downtown Dallas . Both are now being treated at Parkland hospital where no statement has been issued yet as to their condition .' We repeat-"

And so the sickening agony of the Death of a President began. Bulletins and unconfirmed reports instantaneously replaced all programming on the radio dial until a half hour later: "John F. Kennedv is dead. The 35th President of the United States has been assasinated by a sniper's bullet in Dallas, Texas."

Every feeling person cried at some time during the following days. Our families and neighbors. Movie stars. World leaders. Search out the magazines and newspapers again-you'll see it there before you and probably be moved once more to tears.

When Kennedy died, so did the illusions of an enraptured America that shared the promise of the Lyrics that he loved: "Don't let it be forgot, that once there was a spot, for once brief shining moment that was known as Camelot." Our innocence was lost; the self-confidence of our invincibility shattered. We weren't a safe nation anymore. Oswald's act was a signal to the nether-world of primitive instincts, and an unending spree of murder or attempted murder began: Robert Kennedy. King, George Wallace. Malcolm X, Ford. Reagan.

After John Lennon was killed, a younger friend told me as she cried: "You don't understand what he meant to me." Didn't I? Idols, heroes, leaders—Valentino, McArthur, Daley—always and will ever be remembered by those to whom their lives had meaning. Kennedy's?

In Sunday's Parade magazine, his brother Ted said in an article, THE SPARK STILL GLOWS: "Last spring, my son Patrick and I visited an island off the coast of Panama, which is home to a desperately poor tribe of San Blas Indians. They have a tradition of naming their children after someone they admire, and on that island we met scores of JFKs, some only 2 or 3 years old. A generation later, in this distant place where few understand English, Jack is still a hero."

Why this lasting devotion? Seldom had one person ever inspired people to positive action for imaginative goals with an eloquence defining his purposes

John Fitzgerald Kennedy

35th President of the United States
Born May 29, 1917
Inaugurated January 20, 1961
Died November 22, 1963

based on sympathy, affection and warmth: The New Frontier, his brief administration was called. All understanding of every human need, it seemed: The Latin American Alliance for Progress; Medicare; The Civil Rights Act; The Peace Corps; The War on Poverty; The Test Ban Treaty. And this admixture of all the elements could also say:

I leaned across the asparagus and asked her for a date."

(Meeting Jacqueline Bouvier, Time, 1957)

"I got a wire from my father that said. "Dear Jack. Don't buy one vote more than necessary. I'll bedamned if I'll pay for a landslide." (New York, 1960)

"Mr. Nixon may he very experienced in kitchen debates. So are a great many other married men I know." (Virginia. 1960)

"There is no city in the United States in which I get a warmer welcome and less votes than Columbus."

(Ohio Dinner. 1962)

"When power corrupts, poetry cleanses, For art establishes the basic human truths which must serve as the touchstones of our judgement... If art is to nourish the roots of our culture, society must set the artists free to follow his vision wherever it takes him." (Speech at Amherst. 1963)

And then .. .

Click, Click. Click. Pulls of a trigger. Yank a flower out of the ground and it will never live again, even if you just as quickly try to force its roots back into the soil. The deed was done.At once we felt the immense loneliness of all people who ever lived since creation when the person who was the repository of all their feelings died.

To those harlots who only try to scandalize his name now, Mark Anthony said of Caesar, "You all did love him once, not without cause; what cause withholds you then to mourn for him?"

Many people have saintly qualities, though I haven't met a saint yet on earth, have you? And has a scale, a measure been perfected yet? that grades our wrongdoings?

If these panderers in print forgot or choose to overlook the overwhelming goodness of this man; if it could be considered so, they should remember that the bullet that shattered his brain was the greatest recompense a man could give for any human frailty, And his sins should be forgiven him.

I took this photo in 1964 of President Kennedy`s first gravesite . I found it humble and befitting a man loved by so many people . Members of various branches of the Services would place their hats there in tribute . Beyond the fence the permanent site with an eternal flame is being worked on that would be dedicated in 1967 . The Lincoln Memorial and Washington Monument are in the distance . The President had once commented about the view from that location

Tom Dimas isn't here anymore

-his Restaurant's
an
architect's office
now

drafting tables
where
booths
used
to
be

the
Gentle Greek
with
Steel wool
Hair

Victor mature
Lips
Scorched
like
Counter top
burns
from
years of serving food
with smokes
dangling
from
his
mouth
"Here's your dinner, Butch,"

(his
Johnny Cash
voice
resonated
like tapping
on a
solid
oak
wine barrel)

"- how's your father today?"

"he's sleeping in the cemetery
next to you, Tom," I thought

St. Mary's
is
across
the
tracks
from
Evergreen

Like the
Quality Diner
Was
separated
by
31st St
from
Pa's
Real Estate
Office.

I was influenced by Edgar Lee Masters' blank verse poem style and 'voices from the grave' in his marvelous "Spoon River Anthology."

My father's real estate office was originally at 3030 S. Wentworth. (He is standing 4th from the right.)

The street became the exit for the Dan Ryan Expressway to 31st Street.

He eventually relocated to the southwest corner of 31st and Parnell.

The Quality Diner was on he next corner at 31st and Wallace. Dimas became my fathers' customer and (mine also) very good friend. His first business was with his brother John and sister-in-law Eva, above left, Tom on the right, the original Kopper Kettle ice cream parlor, pictured here in 1926. It was on the opposite side of the street from the restaurant. The Depression forced its closing in the 1930's. (Dimas's grandson said that the Tom Tom Tamale Co. Started in the same building.)

Poems

THREE POINTS

years
too
late
for
kicking,
retired
men
on
benches
watch
a
spread-armed
boy
head
down
boot
coffee can
field goals
over
the
Healy
schoolyard
fence .
John Aranza

"IS THIS WHAT WE SENT YOU TO SCHOOL FOR?"

mother toed
crumpled papers
I threw on the floor
while trying to
write a poem.
"Uh," I shrugged
how to explain that
one winter day
in Composition 101
an old Mrs. Walsh
glanced out the
18th floor wifldow
at De Paul and said :
" 'furious white bumble bees'
that's how a poet
once described
swirling snow;
- and listen to this,"
(no one listened then)
opening a dog-eared book on her desk:
" 'he brushed the velvet,
but the crumbs jumped
impishly up and down.'
Isn't that beautiful too?"
she stared out again at the
storm, wiping her eyes.

John Aranza

THE CHICAGO RIVER AT THROOP STREET

is a

shimmering

coat of mail

squinting

silver and grey

at a

furious

white-hot

sun.

The trombone blast

of a

tug boat

startles

pheasants

from

mistaken

prairies

of

wreckers' yards

into

wings of

Oriental

Rugs -

through

loose green

sequins

of

dangling

poplar leaves

like thousands of

faces

in a

nervous

stadium crowd

chanting

"Hurry, hurry, hurry, hurry, hurry."

By John Aranza 31

DOWNTIME

Gym shoes
tied together
by their laces
seem forever
hanging from
neighborhood
utility wires.
Flung up
there by
some
goofy
ferris-wheel-armed
kid
who
didn't
know how he'd
get those
Converses
down
once he
horse-shoed
'em on;
- or
that one day
he'd be moody
on someone
else's pair
to be
goofy
ferris-wheel-armed
again.

John Aranza

The Lost Theatres of Bridgeport

Chicago has always been a city of neighborhoods and churches. And within our Bridgeport, a neighborhood was usually the circle of influence of your parish and the blocks surrounding it—whether, say, Holy Cross, St. George's, Doremus or St. Anthony's-and then the commercial streets enclosing you, and the blocks your ethnic groups occupied, such as 26th St., 31st, Halsted or Morgan.

And as much a part of the little-town effect of your church, corner butcher shop and bakery was the neighborhood show. We all had the Ramova for the popular movies as soon as they came from the Loop, but our small, nearby shows, most no wider than 25 foot storefronts, were first the inexpensive elixirs of life for newly-arrived immigrants, then school-aged children and Depression and war-burdened neighbors. And Vilma Banky, Herbert Marshall and Douglas Fairbanks were as evocative and important to those generations as Jacqueline Bisset, Robert Redford and Harrison Ford is to this one's.

My mother's recollections were about the Normal Theatre when she lived at 2618 S. Normal. It was around the corner from her on 26th Street where Naponiello's Bowling Alley is now. She laughed when she told me how she thrilled to a William S. Hart silent movie as he stared coldly at a villain while firing a 'Pair of six-shooters, in-and-out like the arms connecting the wheels of a locomotive. There was always a piano player there too, she said, below the screen, who would look up and

NOR-WAL THEATRE OPENS FRIDAY, SEPTEMBER 1 AT 6 P.M. CA. 5-7106   518 W. 26th ST.

accompany the action. And during Pearl White Serials (The Indiana Jones of the 1910's and 20's), she became excited and played faster as the action heightened. I know Ma's not mad at me for revealing that part of her, because we all have been thrilled in some forgotten one or two-aisled show.

Irene Brody of St. Bridget's Parish remembers her neighborhood's shows well: "The people north of Archer Avenue usually went to the McCarthy Bros.' Loomis Theatre," she said, "mostly because the children weren't permitted to cross busy Archer Avenue. (The Loomis was located approximately at Bonfield on the north side of Archer, but it was demolished for the Stevenson Expressway). "The Keeley Show," she continued, "was usually patronized by those living south of Archer Avenue. All the neighborhood children looked forward to going to either one on weekends-and for 5 cents to get in." You and I can still see the Keeley at 2839 S. Archer, only in its present use as a warehouse. The glazed bricks and ornamental brackets of the facade are all that hint of what used to be-except for the memories of those who went there.

The Eagle on Morgan Street was an exciting part of that neighborhood, Harriet Lescauskas, the Pharmacist across the street recalls: "They used to line up on the sidewalk to get in." Its name is forgotten behind the NAPA auto repair sign above its former entrance at 3342 South Morgan, but you who lived near there or went in remember, don't you? The Eagle couldn't survive the

FRI. and SAT., MAY 19 and 20
—Double Feature Program—
—Feature No. 1—
A Thrill Sensation!

ADVENTURE!
DRAMA!
WALLACE BEERY ROBERT TAYLOR
STAND UP AND FIGHT
Florence Rice
Chas. BICKFORD
Story of Women,
Men Could Love

—Feature No. 2—
Jane Terrorizes the West!

JANE WITHERS
It's Jane's Favorite Picture!
THE ARIZONA WILDCAT
with LEO CARRILLO
PAULINE MOORE • WILLIAM HENRY
HENRY WILCOXON • DOUGLAS FOWLEY
ETIENNE GIRARDOT

Also NEWS

402—National Program & Printing Co.

—Next Week—
SUN. and MON., MAY 21 and 22

—Giant Double Feature Program—
—Feature No. 1—

The most excitable and lovable
folks you've ever met . . . in a
salty drama.
BOBBY BREEN
Fisherman's Wharf
with
LEO CARRILLO
HENRY ARMETTA
LEE PATRICK
and
SLICKER, The Seal
What a "family"!
What a crew!

—Feature No. 2—

The Adventures of JANE ARDEN
WITH
ROSELLA TOWNE
WILLIAM GARGAN
JAMES STEPHENSON
BENNY RUBIN
DENNIE MOORE

She's stepping RIGHT OUT
OF AMERICA'S FAVORITE
COMIC STRIP
ONTO THE SCREEN!
Plenty of action
with the darling
of the comics
on the screen!

MILDA
3140 So. Halsted St.

Telephone VICTORY 4424
SUNDAY, DOORS OPEN 1:00 P. M.
DOORS OPEN DAILY 6:00 P. M.

PROGRAM—STARTING MAY 14

SUN. and MON., MAY 14 and 15
Double Feature Program—No. 1
Numbers Racket Exposed!

MURDER for 8,000,000¢! . . . "Numbers racket"
exposed! Gangland guns a'roar in the dynamite drama
of a one-man war on
the mob making mil-
lions in policy-slips!
RICHARD DIX
TWELVE CROWDED HOURS
with LUCILLE BALL
ALLAN LANE

—Feature No. 2—
A New Hopalong Adventure!

EXCITING THRILLS . . . as the trail-
blazers race across the range into
double-barrel action!
Clarence E. Mulford's
THE FRONTIERSMEN
A Paramount Picture featuring
WILLIAM BOYD
with George Hayes • Russell Hayden
Evelyn Venable • Clara Kimball Young

— Added —
NEW EPISODE OF "THE LONE
RANGER RIDES AGAIN"
News Events

TUESDAY, MAY 16
—One Day Only—
Family Night with a Special Show
All Balcony Seats 10c
All Main Floor Seats 15c
DOUBLE FEATURE PROGRAM—Feature No. 1
A South Sea Drama!

Thundering Thrills and Flaming Romance
on Savage South Sea Islands!
RED MORNING
with
STEFFI DUNA
REGIS TOOMEY
RAYMOND HATTON
Pagan fires burned in
her breast . . . but the
white man's love was
in her heart.

—FEATURE No. 2—
Music and Romance!

Song-drenched romance to
warm your heart.
HOORAY FOR LOVE
A Star-
Glittering
Musical
Romance
Ann SOTHERN
Gene RAYMOND
Bill Robinson, Maria Gambarelli
Thurston Hall, Pert Kelton

WED. and THURS., MAY 17 and 18
DOUBLE FEATURE PROGRAM—No. 1
An Epic o the Railroads!

Love written in rousing drama as
they defy the Wall Street barons
LET FREEDOM RING
Nelson Eddy
with Virginia Bruce
Victor McLaglen
Lionel Barrymore
Edward Arnold
Guy Kibbee
"A new high
in reckless
love!"

—FEATURE No. 2—
The "Woo Woo" Fun Is On!

WOO! WOO!
They're enough to
drive even a sane
man crazy!
HUGH HERBERT
The FAMILY NEXT DOOR
JOY HODGES
Eddie Quillan • Ruth Donnelly
Juanita Quigley • Benny Bartlett

Added—"THE MARCH OF TIME"

Free to Ladies—22-KARAT HAND-
DECORATED CHINAWARE
Especially Designed for Milda Theatre

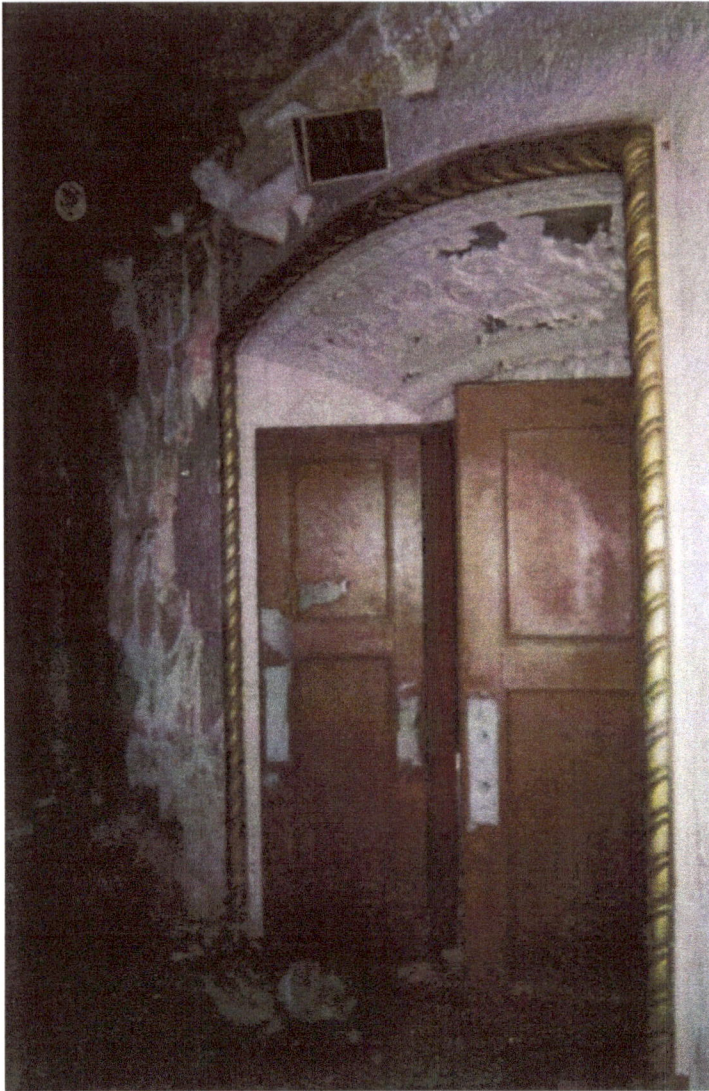
Entrance way to the past. Ramova. Aisle3.

"This way to your seat, please."

early lure of T. V.— even with the giveaways of the last owner, Morris Zimmerman-and like the Keeley, it closed in the 50's.

My neighborhood theatre was the Wallace Show at 622 W. 31st St., a bicycle shop now. Originally owned by the Balaban and Katz Corp., it too was a silent movie show first. (Ellen O'Brien of the long-time area residents Richardson family played piano and organ below its screen flickering with Valentino and John Gilbert).

We remember Bill Aslanides and his harried sons trying to keep order among us scrambling children. Our neighbor Gerri Destefano's rememberances are evidenced by the Godey plates in her pantry that were give-a ways. But T. V., and sadly, the changing habits of all of us away from our once faithfully-attended show saw it too close in the early 60's.

The same dis-use closed the Metropole— now Val's Dance Studio at 238 W. 31st St.-the Lithuania, whose name is perpetuated in the mosaic-tiled entrance to the Bridgeport Hardware Store at 3214 South Halsted Street, and a lost strand of pearls recalled by our Historian on Halsted St., Stanley Gapshis, that was the Marian (now the New Deal Liquors at 3450 S. Halsted), the Monogram (now Granato's Bakery at 3520 S. Halsted) and the Casino-now a newspaper called the Bridgeport News at 3506 South Halsted Street.

Even now, the once-elegant Milda, which quietly awaits an uncertain future behind the yet-completed offices at 3142 S.Halsted St., is lost in Time's changing ways. Our home-grown neighborhood architect, Ron Vari, said: "The lore is that an apprentice of Louis Sullivan designed the Milda, only one of two theatres with his influence." Gone forever is the glitter of Vaudeville from its stage, 'fashion contests with audience participants, live dramas, Dish Nights, pie-eating contests (that Peter Maniates of David's once won because his cousin kept pushing his face down into blueberry pies that he really disliked), live orchestras and the Three Stooges pranking only across the screens of our memories now. Lost too is the marble statuary at the entrance of this theatre once managed by Nick Konstantelos (as his brother Gus managed the Ramova) and the marquee that blinked in pastel lights like a pulsating stained glass.

…and yet-like all fallen idols-a once-popular president voted out of office; a mini-skirt no longer in vogue'; last year's anything, or a 1920's styled building we call old fashioned- nothing seems to keep our loyalty forever. We can lament the passing of those 'lost' theatres, but didn't we all in some way cause it? It was nice being in those eras, but we don't live there any more. Or as Thomas Wolfe wrote: "You can't go home again ... to the escapes of Time and Memory."

... and yet, still, can we ever recreate the oil and salt smell of the hot popcorn that permeated the entire show after popping furiously like muffled firecrackers in those little machines in the lobbies? Or does memory just make it seem that it can't be so again either?

By John Aranza 35

"Hooray For Hollywood"

Last week, those young reporters Anna Aranza and Irene Brody referred to a few shows in "The Lost Theatres of Bridgeport" by their nicknames. The 'Normal' was actually the Nor-Wal and the Butler at different times, and the 'Keeley' was the Holden.

While writing about this, something else came to mind: the Ice Cream Parlors inevitably located nearby each one of the theatres. Kunka's, close to the Loomis and the Holden; David's, by the Milda; Floodas' near the Ramova; the Kopper Kettle by the Wallace Show; Kupshas' next door to the Eagle, and how many others closed and forgotten?

EAGLE Theatre

Telephone YArds 7-4434   3324 So. Morgan St.

WED. & THURS., AUG. 2nd-3rd
"Love at First Bite"
3 Stooges
LADY GODEY
Dinnerware to the ladies

CAROL REED'S PRODUCTION
THE 3RD MAN

COMING! DAN DAILEY ANNE BAXTER
A TICKET TO TOMAHAWK
20. Color by TECHNICOLOR

FRI. & SAT., AUG. 4th-5th
"The Vicious Years"
"Name-O-Luck"
SAT. NITE 8:30
New Serial Chapter 2
"ATOM MAN vs. SUPERMAN"

SUN.-MON.-TUES.
AUG. 6-7-8
"The Asphalt Jungle"
Sterling Hayden, Louis Calhern

Gregory
PECK as
THE Gunfighter 20.
with MILLARD MITCHELL • Directed by HENRY KING • Produced by NUNNALLY JOHNSON

Then I thought of my friend and Irish wit, Bobby Green, and his philosophic statement: "What goes around, comes around." Although Sweet Dreams and the Neon Rainbow on 31st St., and Scoops on Halsted aren't thought of in the traditional manner, as being identified with Shows, the recurrence of these welcomed candy shops or ice cream parlors in the neighborhood give one meaning to Bob's saying.

In the poignant movie, "The Last Picture Show," the Royal, in a drab-looking but interesting Texas town, was a one-aisled show I know we all could identify with by substituting the neighborhood theatres of our youths:

"Coming Soon" cases at the sidewalks with gaudy-colored posters, and in the narrow outer-lobbies, those magical popcorn machines and a cracked glass candy counter filled with Good and Plenties, Ju Ju Beads and Milk Duds. The aisles leading us within, were tacky as fly-paper from spilled pop and ground-in candy over the years, taking us more often to a broken seat sloping downwards to the floor-which we completely forgot if we enjoyed the feature or the one we were with.

I'm not trying to get personal, but didn't you have more than a few dates that included sitting in a not-to-bright part of the show? Or, as a more innocent child, did you "Giddy-up" down the street after watching a Western if you were a boy (they imitate the sounds of laser beams now). And if a girl-well, I admit I can't imagine what seeing Shirley Temple, Hayley Mills or Carrie Fisher meant to you.

I do know we all agree that movies were- and still are- a vital part of our lives. Yet as much as I enjoy them, I had difficulty getting the 'feel' of some popular, newer youth-oriented films.

Your author at work researching. The old Lithuanian Auditorium, Chicago

Watching my nine year old son being fascinated by "Star Wars" and "E.T." recently, I commented to my wife, Elaine, sitting on the other side of me : "These could be great movies but there's something missing." And I kept watching Johnny Boy staring motionless, as this creature that looked like a leathery turtle tried to say: "El - eee - ut."

"John," she whispered to me, "-it's you."

And then I realized, that like the ending of Victor Herbert's song, "Toyland"-once you pass its borders, you can never go back again.

The Night the Pied Piper Came to Bridgeport

You don't believe in Fairy Tales? "The Invasion of the Body Snatchers", either? (Original version, please.) Oh. Wow, to use the current vernacular.

Well. He was here. At a street dance, one night in August, 1956. It was one of those quickly planned events that become memorable for a lifetime. An impulsive fun-thing, only young people in the unlimitable imaginations can conceive. Like a Busby Berkeley, Depression-era musical: "Hey gang, let's put on a show."

We received a Permit to block 30th Street between Parnell and Wallace. From a porch on the north side of 30th and the garage on the south side behind the food store, where we sold hot dogs and pop out of, we focused lights onto a square we roped off in the middle of the street.

We? Myself and some childhood friends. Ron Orden, Tom Casale, who worked at the store, and his brother, Joe—may he have sweet peace forever—our Elvis look-alike, who was a showman in a way, himself; who made it easy for us to flirt with all the girls. Joe had long hair and sideburns like Elvis' that fell evocatively over his forehead. And all I had to do was walk ahead of him and clear the way through imaginary crowds, saying" "Step aside, please. Let him pass. PLEASE stand aside." And girls would see the similarity and sense the make-believe and scream a little: "—it's Elvis." And Joe would stretch out his arms until his wrists extended past his jacket's cuffs and begin to comb his hair—and we'd all begin rapping.

In a week, we'd 'sold' the event by word of mouth. For entertainment, we had Bob Scorzo play the accordion, Rich Slajchert on the drums. (Rich who? He appeared at the Chicago Theatre. Orden, Rich, and I went to see the movie "The Girl Can't Help It" with Jayne Mansfield. And when Little Richard started singing the title song, Slajchert took out his drumsticks and began playing on the metal bindings of the seats.) And Nick Spata was on the saxophone. (He's in St. David's parish now. From as caring as and as talented a neighborhood family I've known.)

Then it just happened. The crowd was there. Old-timers who brought their own chairs to listen and watch all of us. Nameless faces and people now, who I remember in form only, dancing the earthy Tarantella when it was played. Middle-aged couples waltzing on the sand we took from Mark White Park and spread on the street. And we teenagers making our newly-discovered 50s rock-and-roll dance moves to "Honky-Tonk" or the band's version of "Night Train."

And then the Pied Piper took over. After we passed the hat for donations for the band, Nicky Spata led us with his saxophone on a New-Orleans-styled dance through the streets. Like doll cut-outs, strung out and holding hands, we followed him up Parnell Avenue to 31st, stopping and dancing in the intersection. Then he led us to Wallace, where a squad pulled up beside him. He blew high-pitched squeaks at the car that he loved to play and create in his songs, like the old factory whistles that used to sound in the neighborhood; and the policeman inside laughed and so did Nicky by making his eyebrows raise—because he kept on playing, with his cheeks puffed out and eyes bulging like a child holding his breath. We paraded down the middle of Wallace Street, and into McCarthy's Day Nursery yard where the surprised owner had guests that night, and then back into the street where we stepped aside as the Wallace-Racine bus came up behind us at 30th. Nicky blew for the smiling driver and passengers, but like all hurricanes that can't keep their force up endlessly, he stopped playing and we walked quietly back along 30th St., as the magic disappeared.

I used to wonder how we "projected" to people outside the neighborhood, but I don't anymore. We know we're scru-

Nickey Spata was an exuberant Bobby Darin look-alike. Typical of Ethnic immigrant families. The children were encouraged in the arts. His brother Joe sang light opera; Luciano self-taught on the piano. Nicky self-taught on the drums and saxophone. Growing up next door to my childhood home at 3021 S. Parnell, the Spatas taught me and the neighbors about opera. fig trees. tomatoes and family The neighborhood was lesser after Nicky died. in 2008

tinized because of our fortunate, political heritage, but beyond that—and we know we're more than that, too—the Poles and the Irish, and the Italians and the Germans, Greeks, Mexicans, Croatians, Bohemians, Jews, Chinese, phew, Who Made this Salad?—we're a unique blend. And—Oh. Wait a minute. My old radio's working again. Ooh—I want to listen to this song. I'll talk to you again soon: "… wa-one, some-mer nye-eye-ite, We fell in luh-uv, (Do, do, do, doom…)"

By John Aranza 37

Bring In the Lady Clown

Besides those at the Ringling Brothers Circus that just opened at the Amphitheatre, and the vocalist of the melancholy song—there is one in our neighborhood that was born, raised, and still living among us who was one of the few female clown performers in the circus world then. (She wants to be known for what she was—not who she is—so I won't identify her.)

"You were really a clown?" I asked, amazed.

"—Wait a minute, John, I want to show you something." She went into the basement of her modest cottage, and she came up with two scrapbooks and a collage of pictures in a 2'x4' frame. Here was a 40 year old mother nonchalantly turning pages of showbills, articles, and mementos at a Bridgeport kitchen table.

Her pictures of over 20 years ago affirmed her to me. In one, the wide stiff-mesh collars we associate with all clowns was really there beneath her chin; her face was covered with clown-white makeup, and her cheeks were rouged with circles. And with her heavily mascaraed lashes, she looked like a child playing make-believe with her mother's cosmetics.

"What were you doing here?" I pointed to another pose. She was wearing a gown and holding an umbrella made only of spokes.

"One of my routines; you can't see the sign of my purse saying: WAITING FOR THE RAIN. Another was walking a stiff leash with no dog."

She said it all started after reading The Clown by Emmett Kelly for her high school English teacher who wanted her to discover and enjoy books. "It opened a whole new world for me," she continued. "It appeared to be such an exciting and colorful life. I quit school in the middle of my Junior year, and I worked as a filing clerk while waiting for replies to the 10 or 12 letters I sent out each week to circuses."

I asked if that was the right thing to do.

"—Oh I thought so," she replied seriously. "My home life was sad and depressing. What a contrast it offered to a kid from a cold-water flat. I helped raise my 4 younger brothers and sisters since I was 13

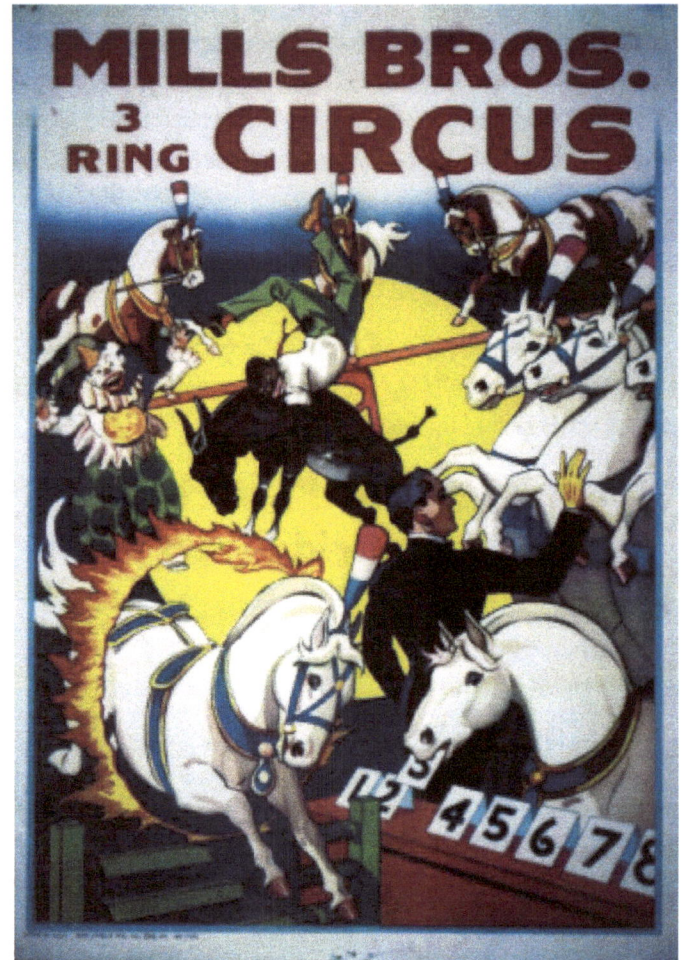

while my parents worked. "I could see the show person in her. Her insightful talk, her expressive facial movements; her love for children she had yet—her 2 year- old son—that she constantly kissed and looked over who was playing near us.

I examined those replies she saved. Envelopes and letterheads of the Bailey Brothers Circus: "That Grand Old Show"; Ringling Bros.; Famous Cole Wild Animal Circus; Mills Brothers 3 Ring Circus—stationary alive with borders of carousel horses, elephants standing of hind legs and roaring lions.

"The Cristiani Brothers Circus hired me when they did 3 Chicago suburban mall shows in 1959. They didn't have schools training you, and I was kinda resented being a girl. But I thought 'This is the Life'; but it really wasn't the life. But I saw it as being very beautiful as it was. Making children laugh. The sheers we wore; and the big bugle beads," her eyes opened widely; "and over-sized hats," she gestured.

"—why didn't you stay with it?" I asked.

"By 23 I lost my taste for it. It was a shiftless life for me. Most of the acts were families that lived together. I'd stay in a motel or as I had to occasionally, in the back of a partitioned truck that transported 3 bears that flopped about. I slept and changed in the back," she laughed, "but I began to miss my family and friends and the neighborhood. So I came home and worked again—at Dressels—in Loop department stores. I even led the State Street Parade once in my costume."

"Any regrets," I wondered.

"I actually met Emmett Kelly, and he told me before I started: 'Don't do it. It's a sad life.' And it is. Performers are talented and serious, but sad people too. But something I learned: Don't ever not try something that is good. My own mother was sad all her life that she wasn't a dancer. So don't let your life get away; don't put your dreams in a drawer. When I see all the young kids hanging out on 31st Street, I wish they'd begin reading and discover themselves too. I hope they read this in the Bridgeport News. There's a big world out there. Even if you try and fail; it's not to try and fail that's a disaster. Even though something was meant to be, you'll never know unless you try."

She told me she took her GED test 4 years ago, and that she's studying to be a nurse: "But that chemistry I have to take," she shuddered "—I want to make sick children better and happy now."

Well, I thought as I left her, she's probably always making others feel that way, and another song came to mind:

"—oh When the Saints go Marchin' In, She's gonna be in that Number, When the Saints go Marchin' In."

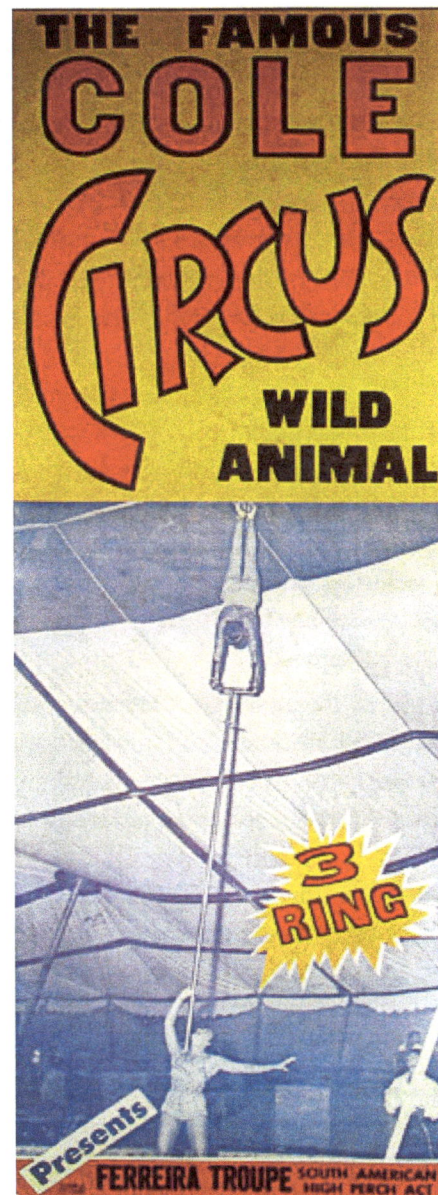

By John Aranza 39

Visit to a Small Planet

On our way to an outing at White Pines Forest as teenagers, my boyfriends and I stopped in mid-state Sycamore for coffee. Instead of "-what'll ya have?" the waitress began: "Did'ja hear? Sycamore beat Plato Center last night. Sycamore beat Plato Center." Ah Basketball. The pride of little town lives.

And how would we ever know about Kewanee, Bushnell, Cobden, Shawnee or Pinckneyville if the state basketball tournament didn't bring all the Main Streets of Illinois into our living rooms once a year on Channel 9 with their infectious, innocent hysteria?

While working on my 25th Anniversary Alumni Banquet from De La Salle 2 years ago, I rediscovered the little town among us, staying for a game after calling my classmates from the school office. And I've been back often, since.

The Meteors were playing the Wolfpack at one of last month's home games.

High on the wall behind the west bleachers, banners proudly proclaimed the school's recent victories, like the Crusaders returning from the Holy Wars:

1977-3rd Place IHSA Tournament. 1978—Catholic League Champs. 1979—Catholic League Champs and Elite 8. 1980-Catholic League Champs. 1981-82-Catholic League Champs. ("Hamlet, Buffalo Prairie, Flatville." I thought of unheralded towns lost in the small print of my Illinois roadmap, waiting for their glory.)

I sat in the stands with squirming St. Ignatius and De La Salle students, of course each certain which team was going to win. (Those same stands where Wally Chodor and I would sneak a cigarette at lunchtime in the long ago '50's, blowing the smoke downwards as if cooling ourselves; and while sitting hunched-over, fanning the cigarette in a flipper-like motion near our ankles, trying to thin out the smoke.)

And weren 't the proud parents there? The Miloslavichs and Aunt Caroline of St. Jerome's, watching for their Frankie to play in " D's" varsity game, and Kathy LoCoco with her son Nick, who just finished playing on the freshman team.

(None of them, I felt, knowing what the fawning was about until they'd be parents one day.) The Ciarvinos from Wells Street were watching their daughter Gina cheerlead, and Ken Zekich from Emerald Avenue more cautiously watched his girlfriend Jan Botica cheerlead too. And over there State Senator Degnan's son was playing for St. Ignatius. (Here was our Main Street, I thought, and all of its citizens.)

In front of me down on the floor, as befitting a Patriarch, Chet Bolger sat in a folding chair at half court. "D's" long-time football coach, the former Chicago Cardinal great, who lives quietly retired at 37th and Winchester. " Hi Coach.- hey Chet, how're ya?" the recognition went on and on with the passing fans.

My niece Debbie Kudulis was with me, with her girlfriends Amy Donovan and Leslie Shurla. Well- for a while at least. Until she spotted something far more interesting away from me: "Oh Unc, do you mind if we sit over there?" As if over there was unimportant and meaningless. "Sure Deb" I released her, thinking of how me and the neighborhood guys socialized with girls at the games back then.

Behind me, this small town's living folklore, the Niego brothers, were talking to their still-faithful admirers. Charles and Tom, the twins, playing for Lewis College now, and Joseph, a freshman there with them. Stars at "D" who took them to the recent championships. (And their fourth brother on this year's team.) So polite and friendly, almost "Aw shukin' " to the adulation as they visited. And near them, Dan Burich another recent neighborhood "D" star, now playing for Loyola, mixing through the crowd with his friend John Peso.

I almost expected to see Meridith Wilson's Music Man strut through the gymnasium doors, high-steppin and poking his baton into the air, with all of the Brothers and Mothers and Father's Club members volunteer-working that night, clapping behind him.

Damn if I didn't want to start some cheers I remembered, not hearing the fans pick up on any: "Go De La Salle, Go De La Salle, Go De La Salle Go," pounded in my temples.

When the game was over and the spectre of Preston Foster had finished oomp, pah, pahing, the stands were empty and I walked down dusty Main Street to my car at 34th and Wabash.

Who won? You know I was so excited, I don't remember?

But I'll be back at the next home game, and there'll be life once more in all the De La Sallevilles throughout the darkened state.

Yeah team.

I Couldn't Find What I Was Looking For

Early Sunday morning, I took my son with me to De La Salle to find a momento for myself out of the rubble of the original building that's being demolished. Something that would remind me of my years at "D" (1953-1957).

At 35th and Wabash, a security guard was out of his car before I was out of mine. "—uh, I went here.

Help the Alumni Association raise funds. Just looking for something —"

"Go ahead," he smiled, "— lotta guys have been here."

Like trying to scale a mountain, I climbed the toppled limestone blocks that were the ornate, upper front of the school; knocked down to first floor height now, only one column remaining, beginning the arched entrance way.

It's an untelling site, a building being torn down. A clock dropped and burst open; coils irreplaceably sprung out; parts scattered. The upper floors of the half' exposed school a mouth open silently, unable to protest. Windows broken. Hardwood flooring lapping down to nowhere, where the wrecking ball smashed through.

" Aranza. Pick that wad of paper up off the floor — don't throw it. Walk to the wastebasket," I could remember a Freshman teacher cautioning me.

I tried to budge a block I uncovered with vine-

like carvings, "No. 17, Over Front Door," it had an 1890's stone mason's marking on the back of it. Too heavy, so I began examining smaller fragments around me. It had to be something intricate, I thought.

I looked up again at the naked hallways, the sun revealing them now.

Us yet-to-be-formed men started there, "Ducky," "Muffin," "Spider," "Gerks," "Bubbles"; " Griffin, Horsch, Lollock, McCarthy and Evanski." Wearing our father's most outlandish ties when the dress code was first introduced. The Brothers winced, but understood and prevailed. Gradually we bought good ones as we wanted our looks to improve as we became Juniors and Seniors.

Those knowing Brothers. They taught us away from those cracked blackboards I looked at up there, and we didn't even know it. To learn poetry by reciting it for being late, or forgetting those ties. To learn how to socialize, bringing in girl high school students for Symposiums and Plays. To discover ourselves beyond our awkwardness, in sports, the band, the newspaper, the debate team, or that we just couldn't speak out without a purpose.

I was sifting through bricks now where they spilled onto the sidewalk. Where Brother Josephus (Adv. 31,Religion I, Cafeteria, CTA, it said after his name in the yearbook. Drill Instructor, fundraiser, a Dallas Green "gamer," your Hard-hitting Old Man, you could also write in,) ; where Brother Joe (Brother Bus, Riska would call him) would tell us if we hunched off the curb into the street, to be first on the coming 35th Street bus, "Get off the earth. Get off the earth, I said. Back onto the sidewalk."

I went back to my car, at least with the school's street numbers no one took off the building, but still looking around.

The security guard walked back up to me: "Couldn't ya find what you were looking for?"

"Nope," I thought of rehearsing for our Senior Play with our own David Merrick, the late Mr. Lewandowski, and singing at parties afterwards,"- no, I couldn't find the right brick."

Then it was Mayor Richard J. Daley who spoke at the laying of the cornerstone ceremony in 1961 . I wrote the school's Centennial History , 1889-1989 Regardless of your political beliefs , I please hope that you at least agree with the dedication that I wrote to his Honor beneath the picture

He always cast a shadow. And he never forgot his school. The Honorable Richard Daley ('19) Mayor of the City of Chicago. "Why, man, he doth bestride the narrow world Like a Colossus . . . "
Cassius, Julius Caesar,

Mike Hughes:
'On a mission from God'
April 7, 2009

By John E. Aranza | April 2009

John Belushi and Dan Akroyd started their " mission from God on the southeast corner of 91st Street and Burley Avenue in the movie The Blues Brothers .

Canaryville's Mike Hughes began his in 2005 on the opposite corner at Our Lady of Guadalupe School.

Before that, Hughes had a storied career at De La Salle Institute in Bridgeport: instructor, head football coach, and assistant principal at De La Salle during the 1980s. He is a La Sallian and Honor Key Award recipient, past-president of the De La Salle alumni association, committee member of the Bulger Stadium project, and still active in school affairs. Many members of his extended family attended the Bridgeport high school as well.

His connection with Our Lady of Guadalupe started when the pastor, the Rev. James Maloney, contacted Hughes, whose name was on a list of recommended administrators and teachers from the Archdiocesan office, and offered him the position of principal.

During the interview process, Fr. Maloney said to Hughes, "The job is perfect for you."
Only after Hughes had signed the contract did the pastor tell him, "Well, lad, we have challenges" and reveal that he was retiring and leaving.

Hughes had a confirmation hearing with Auxiliary Bishop Joseph N. Perry. During a subsequent meeting in summer 2005 with Bishop Perry, the Archdiocesan schools superintendent, and accountants, Hughes was asked instead to oversee closing Our Lady of Guadalupe School. Enrollment totaled 31, and it appeared there was little chance to attract enough students for the fall to make the school viable.

Mike Hughes worked to keep Our Lady of Guadalupe School open when it was in danger of closing. (Photo by Troy T Heinzeroth)

Hughes pleaded for at least six months to try to keep the school open. "I preferred to inject enthusiasm and continue what had begun many years before," Hughes said.

The fact that six surrounding South Chicago parishes had closed their schools did not deter him. Neither did the fact the school operated in a low-income area, in which 90% of the area students qualified for free or reduced lunches based on Federal guidelines.

Hughes spoke at every Mass, walked the neighborhood, and knocked on doors.

"The challenges are many, but the potential incredible," Hughes said.
Principal Mike Hughes of Our Lady of Guadalupe School helps third grader Victor Herrera on during Crazy Hat Day, one of the many activities that take place during Catholic Schools Week. (Photo by Troy T Heinzeroth)

By John Aranza 43

He contacted the Big Shoulders Fund, set up by the late Cardinal Joseph Bernardin to tap into financial assistance from corporate leadership to help inner city schools.

The referral Hughes received from the fund was a successful Indiana businessman whose football idol was Mike McGill, a two-way middle linebacker/fullback who, before he played for Notre Dame and the Pittsburgh Steelers, played for Bishop Noll High School, where he ran at—and sometimes over—De La Salle football player Mike Hughes in the early 1960s.

"Things just came together," Hughes said, after the painful (for Hughes) sharing of memories of McGill endeared the donor to Hughes's needs.

That year, supporters pledged $100,000, with like amounts pledged for each of the next four.

Hughes's walking, talking, and a lifetime of commitment to youngsters is what really came together. He personally kept the school open and upped the enrollment to 170, with larger enrollments projected.

The basement gym and activity center was restored—along with community confidence in the school.

Since 2005, Hughes has overseen more than $800,000 in building and capital improvements. Test scores rank consistently above national averages. All graduates in recent years have been accepted to top private and Catholic schools. Seven of the Class of 2008 moved along to De La Salle.

Hughes is not the only Our Lady of Guadalupe hero. Twelve parishioners were killed in Vietnam, more than from any other parish in the United States. Today, 114 are on active duty in all branches of the services. Nobody at Guadalupe is a stranger to challenge and courage.

It has been a long time since young Mike Hughes, oldest in his family of 11, was fascinated by the bustling world of the stockyards alongside his Canaryville neighborhood as he walked from his St. Gabriel's Parish to play at the Valentine Boys and Girls Club more than a mile away.

For the grown Mike Hughes, much still seems to be seen with child-like wonderment and possibilities.

Thanks to him, the challenged area of Our Lady of Guadalupe is being taught to see with the same eyes, too.

Principal Mike Hughes of Our Lady of Guadalupe School helps third grader Victor Herrera on during Crazy Hat Day, one of the many activities that take place during Catholic Schools Week. (Photo by Troy T Heinzeroth)

I Remember Michaeleen Kudulis

I thought that waiting for time to pass since Mikey died on November 30, 1982 would soften the hurt: make this easier to write. It didn't, and I knew better. My father died 20 years ago, and not a day passes that I don't think of him in different ways.

All of you are recent member of the sad fraternity of those left behind and you understand the loss I speak of. And though I realize Michaeleen death is more deeply felt by the family and her friends than the world knows—just as the death of one of yours can't possibly be felt with the same intensity by others— what it meant to those she left behind, represents us all.

Forty. Wife. Mother of four. Daughter of parents still living. Sister. Keeper of a menagerie—Fluffy, Shep, and "Prince the Wonder Dog," as she affectionately called him. A touch of class in her clothes that mirrored her soul. Waitress at Mr. Christopher's. Full-time Supervisor at Midas International. Bunco player.

As I sat in St. Jerome's Church the day of the funeral mass, I thought that if strongest among us could fall, how vulnerable the rest of us are. And when the funeral cars made their slow way through the neighborhood Saturday morning, life on 31st Street and around her home at 29th and Canal was routinely doing its needed tasks, while we inside those insulated cars could only numbly stare out, or within ourselves, with grief.

"Why, Uncle John," her fifteen year-old daughter asked me, "why did God take Mommy away before she even finished raising us?"

"God love you, Tamara, but she was. If you could ask that question with no bitterness, as you did, your mother was a success." But that doesn't explain death or its meaning, or take away the hurt, I know.

You Aunt Elaine wakes up in the middle of the night agonizing. I'm sure that Delores upstairs and Jo next door and how many more; none of us are aware what to do, too.

Michaeleen is an angel now, and we can only conjecture in human images what Heaven is like.

I want to think that your Mommy has her hair done by Cherubs that constantly accompany her. That she's the talk of the Universe with rings and jewelry that even God permits because she's so precious. And that she moves about painlessly in soft grass, with little puppies and their runny noses nudging at her feet and jumping up to be petted by her consoling hands.

The Birthday Party

Last Tuesday, my sister Mary, my wife, my mother and I went to Emily Krstulovich's (Rosner's) wake, a neighbor who most of you don't know. She used to live at 30th and Parnell, where the new Healy School is now.

Emily was in her early fifties, the same age as Mary, her very good girlfriend. Outside of her family and friends, her death will be as unmomentous as the hundreds of other that occur each week in Chicago. That can't be helped.

If you're like me, you have friends that you may not have seen for years, but when you meet again, it's as if no time had passed at all. It was like that between Mary and Emily and some of their childhood friends Mary saw at the wake the night before.

"Gootchie," my sister kept repeating in the car on the way to the chapel, "there was Dorothy Houlihan and Martha Zuro and Emily and Lila De Witt," she sing-songed some of those names as easily as I could my childhood friends': Weasel, Flash, Minnow, Eddy Spaghetti.

"We formed a club and called ourselves the Debutanters," she laughed to herself, recalling something for the first time in years.

"Once, we were at the Bucket of Blood.

(The New National Ballroom at 33rd Place and Morgan nicknamed because of prideful, ethnic arguments (yes, I'll say it, fist fights) at wedding receptions held there. It was also seen in the movie "Only the lonely" with John Candy and Ally Sheedy as the exterior of the funeral chapel and her apartment above. The interior

By John Aranza 45

scenes were at Pomierski's at 32nd & Aberdeen.)

I think it was Lila's turn at watching the purses as the others danced. When someone asked her to dance, she became excited and left them. Sure enough, they were stolen with our keys and money inside. Were the parents' mad," she laughed at it now. "We were crazy." I knew what she meant.

Then I thought of Mary's Sweet Sixteen birthday party. Another life, it seemed. 1944. I was only five, but I can still remember the instant a picture was taken with her friends around her. I was hiding under the dining table, and then I crawled into the bedroom and peeked around the doorway at them.

Young girls. Giggling. Many with hair-dos like the Andrew Sisters with high waves in front.

"Shignons. Rats," Mary described them; the cotton fillers that allow them to form buns or pompadours in their hair.

That long-ago picture. How it always showed up when my mother brought the photo albums out.

Adolescent women, they were. Faithful around Mary in two-toned spectator pumps; flowers and ribbons and feathers in their hair; blouses or jackets with padded shoulders; and alluring, dark red lipstick. "It was Revlon's new color then, 'Fatal Apple'," Mary smiled reminiscently.

And here we were, going to Emily's wake. One of those ever-cheerful faces. "The rose-lipt girls are sleeping, in fields where roses fade," the poet A.E. Houseman wrote.

As sad as Mary was at seeing Emily lifeless there, she was warmed at seeing a few of her old friends, Martha Zuro and Dorothy Houlihan.

I was excited too at seeing them. Before my era's James Dean introduced alienation into the world (and his way was needed) people included others more into their lives; and I was always a part of all my sisters'.

I sensed that other life again. Thirty-eight years ago. I don't know what Martha and Dorothy

would think if I told them that they were matured versions of that scene I remembered so well. Like cameos, soft and warm-looking; becoming whatever they were meant to be.

Since that night, I thought of what seeing them meant to my sister. She's had another lifetime of 10 children, and the wearing down we all feel once we have to leave our childhood behind. Few of us have the power to maintain those lofty highs of youth forever, but the birthday party came to life again because of a death, and I just keep going over it and over it in my mind, especially hoping that it uplifted my sister—though she seldom complains about anything—probably feeling more sorry for myself whenever I think about the inevitable, while I ruminate in and out of the past, like this, at times, for the sustenance it seems to provide.

Permit me your indulgence, please. Joan was taught to play the piano by the School Sisters of Notre Dame while at Saint Anthony`s. She later taught herself to play the organ. At age 14 she became the church`s organist and then the Choir Director. A graduate of the neighborhood`s Saint Mary of Perpetual Help High School and then De Paul University majoring in Music and Education, she was also a Certified Volunteer Nurse`s Aide and a Certified CPS Teacher at the Komensky Schol before her death at age 25 in 1955. For my parents and my two other sisters, part of them died too. For me , also a Benefactor who took me for rides and then sundaes at Kunka`s on Archer Avenue, paid me for shining her furniure with Olde English Furniture Polish, and bought me a blue suede jacket for for the fidgety teenager stopping biting his fingernails . We never forget our losses , do we ?

1. unknown, 2. Mary Aranza (Condic) 3. Alice Kuczinski 4. unknown 5. unknown 6. Martha Zuro 7. Lilian Rosner 8. Dolores(?) Franz 10. Mary Madera 11. Lila DeWitt 12. Joan Aranza 13. unknown 14. Dorothy Houlihan 15. Emily Krstulovich Some of the unknown's are friends of Emily Krstulovich from Kelly H.S.

Members of Saint Anthony De Padua`s choir . Late 1940`s .
Back Row : Emily Krstulovich , Lilian Rosner , (?) , Teresa Horvath , Rosemary Farugia
Middle Row : Josephine Pelligrini , (?) , Mary Madera , (?)
Bottom Row : My sisters , Mary Aranza Condic (who would have 10 childen) and Joan Aranza .

Sonata in G on Morgan Street

I'm not surprised at the Tribune and Times feature writers who keep coming back to Bridgeport in their stories: In search of 'real peoples' bars; chiding or reprimanding us about something-though with a certain admiration; urging mayoral candidates to live here; or trying to uncover a political lament, but fathoming really nothing.

Are we caricatures, unaware of our blemishes? Or are we the city in microcosm? of such stuff as Sandburg wrote in Chicago:

" ... Under the terrible burden of destiny laughing as a young man laughs,

Laughing even as an ignorant fighter laughs who has never lost a battle,

Bragging and laughing that under his wrist is the pulse, and under his ribs the heart of the people."

Where else are there tied-dyed looking gardens as in our back yards, marvelous kaleidoscopes of jonquils and snapdragons-guarded by scarecrows of old shoes on sticks. Do they sit on the front porches of Winnetka, quietly drinking a summer's beer late into the night? Are there Blessed Mother statues in the front lawns of Everywhere? whose same owners will most likely hate you if you don't vote as they do.

Would Antanas Badauskas sit near the front window of a barber shop in another Chicago community business street, intently playing his violin as he does among us? I often passed his narrow shop at 3137 South Morgan St., not unmindful of St. Anthony's choir director Dr. Frank Pellegrini's plea : "John-there 's so much culture in Bridgeport that goes unnoticed."

"You want to write about me? for the Bridgeport News?- me?" he was incredulous when I entered his shop last week: "- why?"

Explaining that I lived nearby on Arch St., and that my enthusiasm was for the story that each of us could be, Antanas sensed that he was talking with his own. (Even old-country fears are suspended when the neighborhood inquires of itself, and he freely told

me whatever I wanted to know.)

Moved from his Lithuanian birthplace because of World War II, he spent several years in "Awe-strile-ee-ah," that stay affected his native, precise accent; and nearly twenty-five years here.

"- and this," I motioned to a sheet music stand with Bach's Sonatas and Partitas for Violins on it.

" Between customers, there's too much time to think. You could get depressed. And when I'm away from it-even for a few days, if I don't practice-you miss so much; you feel that nothing is so valid. It's like not spending productive time." He sat erectly at the edge of one of the few chairs in his unelaborate shop. The back counters for his tools and lotions weren't porcelain-faced or trendy-just painted with a flat paint-but that seemed unimportant.

Antanas. Bald, in his fifties; his dark-framed glasses magnifying his unblinking eyes-portents of his thoughts - which were expressed in carefully spoken phrases: He was significant."I cut hair-that's an art too-to pay the bills, to eat," he replied to my asking why he barbered.

"-and your music, to live?" I asked.

"Yes," he agreed, only after deliberating on my premise. No artist can conceal truths, and he didn't try-couldn't if he wanted to-hide his affection.

He went into a back room and returned with a well-used violin, protectively wrapped in a rayon scarf. He positioned the instrument under his chin, explaining that you must constantly play to develop your techniques. He then began playing, Tartini's Sonata in G, he identified later.

Antanas was standing resolutely; his left hand as deftly urging the strings as the bow in his right that he guided in a delicate to-and-fro motion. His eyes were closed, though the lids were moving imperceptibly, and his mouth was open slightly, miming inaudible murmurs as the music graced him. I could only recognize that the sounds were sweet, resonating in the body of the violin.

Afterwards he told me how he opted to play in a group, but that he also worried that he couldn't perfect his technique playing in intervals. He explained in great detail how Bach's compositions builds up a musician; of the emotions stressed in Mozart and why Mendelssohn's Concerto is great. But he more than once spoke of what he hinted were inadequacies-"I'm not a star, but a bit more than a hobby player. Best not to talk about it; but step up on a stage and let others hear and judge you."

I left more certain of his talent than he; but artists are that way, deprecating their own value, unsure of their worth, confusing it with the seemingly imperfectability of art itself.

I've thought quite often since I met him, that whatever we are-by whosoever's standards - the neighborhood wouldn't be the neighborhood without our Antanases, or Khersti Ahven's Benton House or those plastic statues in the front lawns. And if eras can ever be recorded in their entirely, I hope somehow that all of the nuances of our times will be remembered.

By John Aranza 49

An American Tragedy

It's Sunday evening, October 23, and I just finished watching "A Place in the Sun" on Channel 9, the 1951 movie based on Theodore Dreiser's 1925 novel, "An American Tragedy".

I've seen it quite often, but never has it brought me so strongly and differently into its influence, like the scene focusing on Elizabeth Taylor over Montgomery Clift's shoulder as she brings him into her gravitational pull, with coaxing lips asking him to "tell momma everything."

But that lovely tragedy Hollywood formulated out of Dreiser's much more somber book was welcomed relief to the week of tragedies we're all familiar with. For me, it all started with reading Bob Greene's Tribune column about an out-of-town De Paul Freshman being robbed twice on the same 'L' platform. Then we were all sickened by the murder of Judge Gentile and our Marines in Lebanon.

But when there isn't harmony in a lesser degree within our families or with our neighbors, I thought, how could we act with amazement when the rest of the world seems out of control?—yet we do.

Because our sensitivity to those grander acts is heightened by our awareness of the tragic flaws in all of us, we're constantly trying to conceal or overcome. If we could only begin by making peace with each other. How simple, I reasoned. Then this would be such a loving world.

But after thinking this out, I didn't call my niece I have a misunderstanding with. Let her make the first move, I still persisted. And I didn't allow myself to become too close to one of my neighbors: "Familiarity breeds contempt," I chose a saying to fit my needs, and not a saying I really needed: "Love thy neighbor."

And as much as I thought I sincerely felt for all those victims, as I watched that movie I knew I was becoming attached to its make-believe world; for the first time knowing what it meant to be temporarily freed from this one, and understanding the actors' dilemma and wishing I could help them—yet not coming forward in real life.
I've read Dreiser's book several times, and I re-read

dog-eared pages for descriptions I especially like. So I knew the movie altered it; that the book was more depressing than this was entertaining. That Taylor didn't visit him in his cell to reassure him of her love; she sent him a not-too-personal letter, only saying that she suffered too, and that she wished him freedom and happiness.

And up to now, I've always smugly said I'm not a TV addict. Refusing to get hooked, probably knowing I would if I'd let myself, more so than believing my other reasons when I said it was because TV was so trite or low-level.

Yet here I was identifying with Montgomery Clift in Elizabeth Taylor's arms, really being affected by the melodramatic musical score, sympathizing with him in an at-times corny trial, when at the moment I couldn't or didn't want to sympathize with everyone in the real world anymore; and also thinking is this what we could become when we lock ourselves within our homes at night from each other?

And I realize as I write this, that this is tragic too.

"Whatta Wictory"

I could have written "Sox win, Sox win, Sox win" as this generation of fans seems to want their commentators to hyperventilate, but I prefer the old-timers in the neighborhood saying it with their Old County accents.

Saturday night the White Sox won the Western Division title of the American League. Maybe I've lost the blind fervor of my youth, but I'm holding back my partying until they win the complete American League Pennant after the mini-series with Baltimore, something you real fans feel they will do—what I of little faith only hope can be true.

But Saturday's victory didn't prevent me from enjoying everyone else's frenzy.

And wasn't everything Wunnerful, Wunnerful with all of the players in the locker room after the game? Tom Paciorek who was demanding to be traded in May; who was so critical of Tony LaRussa then, was more effervescent than any of the bubbly being sprayed around as he gushed into Ken Harrelson's microphone: "…and Tony LaRussa is the greatest manager. The greatest."

Then Carlton Fisk finally set aside his mask of Greek Tragedy, squinting through the champagne dripping off of his soaked hair and laughed happily into the television camera: "…Tony really handled the team well, using all 25 players." Was this the same Carlton Fisk? Who was understandably hurt in June when the manager was platooning him while searching for a winning team chemistry. The same Carlton? Who, while he was on that Channel 32 broadcast, could be read at that same moment in Saturday night's edition of the Sunday Times, responding in a feature about how past winners celebrated, saying how he celebrated inwardly.

"What's going on here, Bunky?" you ask.

These men aren't insincere. You were just witnessing the inexplicable mystery that winning effects upon the human situation. Where all misunderstandings aren't forgotten but understood and accepted how they fit into the Whole.

What about the fans?

I didn't want to sleep anyway, with all of the celebrating people from the park passing my home at 32nd and Parnell. Sitting on my front porch, I watched as hundreds of drivers played their horns in victory. All of the passengers were the same, shouting or signaling, with their index fingers: "We're Number 1. We're Number 1." And how many teenagers boasted to me as they walked by: "We've waited 24 years for this." Wonderful nuts. Maybe their moms and dads were waiting; they weren't even born that night of September 22, 1959, that Vic Power grounded the game-ending double-play to give the Sox that Pennant. A game in which a pitcher named Early Wynn gained his 21st win, and the center fielder for Cleveland named Jimmy Pearsall had 3 hits and a pinch hitter named Chuck Tanner struck out earlier in the fifth inning.

Well, I went to 31st Street and witnessed a New Year's Eve in September. Bumper-to-bumper traffic; heads sticking out of sun roofs; people riding on hoods and fenders. An exuberant young neighbor, Whitey Miller, was across the street working a siren while firecrackers were popping at his feet, and sev-

eral cars stopped for passengers to high-five slap hands with guys celebrating at the curb—and the rockets' red glare and bombs bursting in air could be seen over on Canal Street.

I walked back home at 1:30 a.m. happy that everyone was so happy. Me? I'm a different kind of Nut. I've followed so many losing Sox and Bear teams that winning isn't as important to me anymore. So few teams are winners—as so few of us are successful whatever-we-want-to-be in life—that I've taken up pleasure in identifying with the players who may not be on top, but who never give up trying. That takes a very special person and talent too.

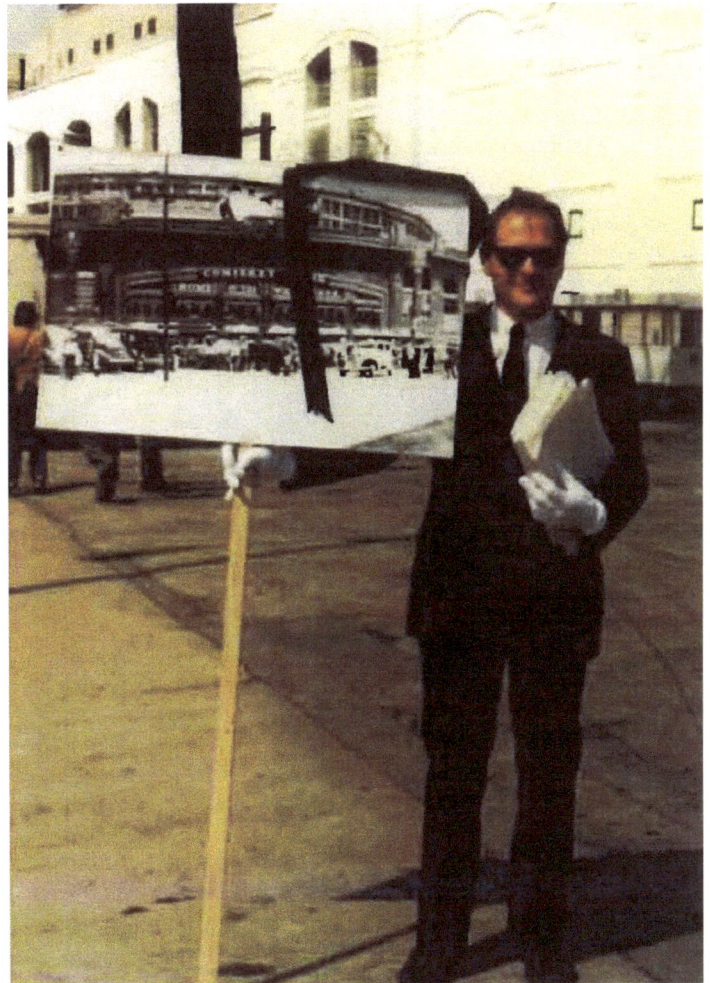

The author dressed as a pallbearer, petitioning the save the historic park 1986.

Out of the park
Detroit News and Free press
May 6,1990

Fans mourn Comiskey, root for Tiger Stadium backers
By E.J. Mitchell II
Detroit News Staff Writer

CHICAGO — John Aranza roams outside Comiskey Park on a cool spring night, as a crowd of White Sox faithful streams into the old Stadium

The ardent Sox fan can hear the roar inside - the announcer's booming voice, the organist's upbeat melody, the rising cheers- but.can't bring himself to push through a turnstile to the ballpark of his boyhood.

Instead, the 50-year-old's gaze wanders across the street, where the American League team will move next year into a new $150-million stadium.

He cringes at the reminder of his lost battle to save the old stadium, built on Chicago's south side in 1910 by Charles Comiskey. Aranza roots for Detroit fans, fighting to save Tiger Stadium. He hopes they never have to face the despair he feels. "I can't bring myself to go in - not now," Aranza said. "I don't know if I will ever go back in. You love it so much, you don't want to go and see it because you know it won't be there next year."

Aranza and other members of Save Our Sox (SOS) came up with a plan to modernize Comiskey Park, but Sox owners Jerry Reinsdorf and Eddie Einhorn refused to meet with the group or consider such plans.

The Tiger Stadium Fan Club in Detroit has met similar resistance from Tiger owner Tom Monaghan over their proposal for a $26.7-million stadium renovation that would add 73 luxury suites, expand restroom and concession facilities and remove some obstructing support posts. But the Tiger Stadium Fan Club still has a fighting chance, said Mary O'Connell, one of Please see Park/10A

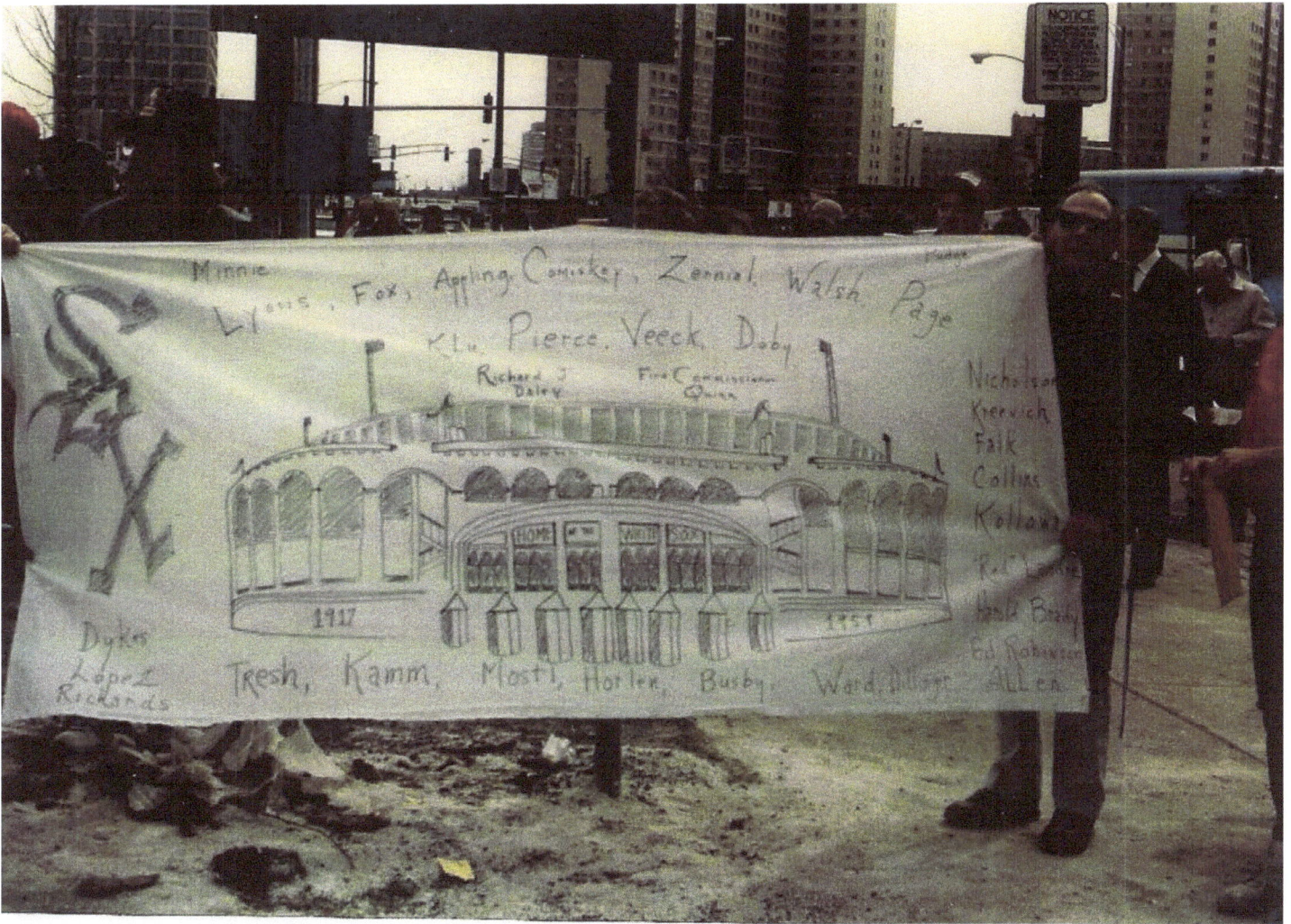

Going to art school paid off. Much to the consternation of my wife, I sketched old Comiskey park on a table cloth with the names of various former Sox players and displayed it on the first day of the demolition of Old Comiskey Park. 1990

"Twilight for the Gods." A Photo that I took of Comiskey's demolition from the new park. 1991.

BRIDGEPORT

SOX

COMISKEY PARK

UNION STOCK YARDS GATEHOUSE 1866

35th
HALSTED

WELCOME
TO
BRIDGEPORT

A Beautiful Neighborhood In

Welcome to Bridgeport
(A fiction)

Sam Romano exited west off the Dan Ryan Expressway onto 31st St. His wife was unconcerned next to him and their eight and six year-old daughters were comfortable in the back seat.

Balich's Drug Store, he noted what used to be Gabric's near Wells St.—that's Croatian too, so this part of the neighborhood couldn't have changed much, he thought.

He drove past Princeton and Shields and under the C&W I RR viaduct to the 'other side of the tracks' into Bridgeport.

"Isn't Sox Park back there?" his wife was curious. "I just wanted to see a little more of the old neighborhood. It's only 6:30—we've got time before the game. And it's been 15 years, you know," he sort of pleaded.

"Daddy," the girls chorused together, "Mommy says the city isn't a nice place. She—"

"It's a wonderful place. It's just that you children didn't know anything about it. Is Daddy a bad man being from here?" He disliked using this tactic, but he knew it was too sophisticated for them to refute.

His wife knew she was trumped for now, and she acquiesced

Scalia's Barber Shop on Canal St.; the Salvation Army on Normal; Brush's Tavern near Parnell. He thought on all the old names the Litany of the Saints.

"Hey—there's Walter Mueller, one of my childhood friends, kids," he directed his joy only to them, "sitting on the mailbox in front of Modern Pharmacy. Hey, Wall," he rolled down his window nans called out. "D—," he began.

"Don't call me that, Samootz," he cautioned.
"Ok, Wally," Sam laughed.
"It figures," he disregarded his wife's remarks, "A forty year-old man sitting on a mailbox in Bridgeport."

He jumped down and walked to them at the curb.
"Wally, why on the mailbox?"
"You suburbanites sit on your patios or in your dens. This is my family room. I guess I never got it out of me."

An old man was walking past; his wide pants flapping like sails. His eyes were reddened, and a dog led him fifteen feet in front of him, leashed by a lifeline of neckties, rope and old belts tied together.
"Chile. Chile Beans," Sam called him.
The old man stopped and stared, trying to remember something through the years.
"Hey, Chile," he handed him $10, "that's for the memories."
"Thank you boy," he slurred on his way, "I no forget you,"
"Sam. You gave him...children, see what I mean?"
"Children," he over-ruled her again, "he lost two sons in World War II and he's never been the same since."
"Wall, is everything still all right here?" He looked at the cast-iron storefronts across 31st St, lined like cans on a grocer's shelf: old, but so much more familiar and welcome than the malls in his O'Hare area. "Where's the Aranzas at; their office is an auto parts store. And Josie's white Horse—it's a candy store. And Dimas' across the street the Greeks' restaurant is a beauty shop now."

"...they're all in the neighborhood yet," his friend reassured him.

"Can we go now?" his wife asked impatiently. "...haven't you seen enough, children?"
They looked amused, but avoided choosing sides: "you said you wanted to see batting practice, Daddy. Is it time for that?"
"Doc, I mean, Wally. Sorry for that. We have to go. It's the first Sox game for them and for me in 15 years. I'll call you, promise."
He pulled away; embarrassed that he didn't even introduce him to his family.
"That's what I mean, Sam," his wife began. "Samootz, Chile Beans, Doc; nicknames and nonsense you've told us for years. And Stinky Lou and Hogjaws and..."
"Mary, Mary," he interrupted her. "Doc is Doc-

By John Aranza 55

bridgeportcoffee™

www.bridgeportcoffeecompany.com

3101 S Morgan, Chicago IL 60608

Tel 773.247.9950
Fax 773.247.9969

For the roastery and wholesale information, please call
773.247.3320

Roastery

3430 S Ashland, Chicago IL 60608

tor Walter Mueller, but he never wanted his neighborhood friends to call him that. Perhaps you read about him in Kup's column last week? He performed the arthroscopic surgery on King Krone's knee of the White Sox. Wally lives somewhere in the neighborhood and likes it that way."

"I didn't know. Who'd think a doctor would—" she stopped.

"We'll just go to the game, and afterwards we'll eat at the Diplomat in Arlington Heights where everyone looks the same and feels safe and talks properly in your old neighborhood."

"Look, Mommy, there's a sign that says 'Leaving Bridgeport. Hurry back.' Are we in another city now?"

"Ask your father, Samootz," she smiled a little grudgingly. "I don't think you can ever leave it."

Close Encounters
of the Nicest Kind

Returning from our recent vacation, my family and I stopped overnight at a motel on Interstate70 in mid-Ohio, about 100 miles east of Columbus.

It would be similar to staying among the farmland communities outside of Chicago or in downstate Illinois: prairie societies with the unsophisticated names of Pleasant City, Crooked Tree and Welcome, hinting at other eras and less complex living.

After a late supper, I said I was going to walk off my bloat by hiking into Old Washington, one such town a mile away. But it was more than just a walk; it was my planned escape from the pinball machines off of the lobby, the TV in the room, and the newspapers on the bed. It was going out where the sensory perceptions are uninterferred with. Just as a radio can receive stations much better at 11:00 pm, the mind can also function more clearly without the static interference of civilization late in the evening.

—there are few earthly solaces such as the solemnic hush of tranquil, less-traveled roads.

The further I walked the blacktop into the enveloping womb of the night; the three-story light standards of the Shenandoah Inn behind me attracting the truckers and cars on the Interstate diminished in importance and became only a fluorescent glow on the horizon.

Stars lit my way now. A description of the English novelist Thomas Hardy about being on a hill on a clear midnight came to mind. That: "…the roll of the world eastward is almost a palpable movement… caused by the panoramic glide of the stars past earthly objects." I focused my eyes on the black silhouette of a nearby barn, and I detected the motion of the universe beyond.

I knew this other world was here, and that's why I sought it out again. That murmur of the firmament overhead. The weathered fence posts and rails. The wild grass encroaching to the shoulder of the road. And the seemingly untroubled lives of the country folk evidenced by screen-doored farmhouses with swings and rockers and flowers potted in old cans on the front porches.

Soon the Big Thoughts came to you: The Meaning of It All. Lost youth. Serenity. Beauty. Your temples and face warm up in exhilaration as from no other experience.

Then the town was upon me. Darkened. Sad. Proud. Lonely. Graceful. Old Washington. Ohio. Population 346. Three blocks of shut-down businesses. Not hastily boarded-up unused stores, but with glass fronts permanently removed and brick or clapboard siding carefully fitted and painted to match the rest of the structures. And they were mostly Colonial-looking buildings that pre-dated the Wild West and the Civil War with empty rooms above that must have been boarding houses years before. Quiet monuments to bygone lives once, most likely, as determined as us to live.

One of the silent structures had 1830 inscribed in a limestone lintel, not that long after the Revolutionary War. The town was a stepping-stone in our country's expansion, but it gave more than just a feel for history; it was as if the hand-formed wood eloquently represented the human qualities of that era.

(I thought of the more recently emptied Jewel Store at Archer and Damen and many of the 'modern' storefronts in the neighborhood—impersonal, efficient-looking structures of tiled floors, suspended grid ceilings and aluminum and brick fronts—and I wondered what impressions they'd give of us to a traveler walking down Halsted Street a hundred years from now after we've all passed away.)

The town still had a Post Office and one store operating, a grocery, but closed for the night, its lights casting a yellow door's image into the street. But the Coke racks and meat coolers inside seemed to infringe here, incongruous in a hundred-year-old building. Modern times did know Old Washington, I thought, and must be eroding its natures. (I've always fantasized that the simple lives of small towns never cultivated big city vices. Of course, the human condition is everywhere, but I don't want to believe it here.)

Our Illinois poet Dave Etter wrote in "Prairie Summer":

Hollyhocks are blooming in schoolyards
Of towns along the Soo Line…

Far off, the lusty wail of diesel horns:
Beef to Chicago, tractors to Omaha.

An older couple met me in front of their home at the edge of town, and I learned that the street I was walking on originally was State Route 40, the forerunner of I-70; then it was relocated and expanded to a block behind town; and then the Interstate a mile away took all the traffic and interest away from Old Washington; from 5 service stations to none. Burger King progress came as close as nine miles away at Cambridge because it was on the new Interstate but Old Washington was overlooked, they said. (Spared, I thought.)

And then they confirmed the ageless dilemma. Most young folk left the town for the big cities, and I explained that some big city folk like myself would welcome the serene life of theirs.

Then the husband looked out past me over the darkened fields and spoke his universal truth: "I spent

a night once at my daughter's townhome in Columbus, and when I woke up in the morning and faced a brick wall, I thought I would die. Don't ever want to be cooped up that way again."

I left them and began walking back to the motel with unreconciled emotions. I knew that I'd be on 31st Street the following day. Back to the familiar and the welcomed, and this would be all behind me. But how could I retain the tranquility of Old Washington on city streets? How can a shell on your desk capture the salt smell of the ocean? Or the lifeless backdrop behind the stuffed animals at the Field Museum imitate nature?

Not even a farm dog that wanted to rip at my ankles spoiled the town's image for me: "What the hail you doin' there, boy," I scared him off in his language. (If he was bigger than the size of a poodle that he was, I wouldn't have talked to him like that.)

But in these Old Washington, Ohio's (or Plato Center, Illinois; or Three Oaks, Michigan; or Rolling Prairie, Indiana) a Presence and Order, a Maker of All Things, the silence we assume without being told to when we enter the reading rooms the Public Library, is sensed late at night when all other earthly activity is quieted; and Something is attempting to soothe the discord in us, appealing to other than our workday selves, to the restless yearnings God implanted in all of us—perhaps giving glimpses of eternity—and fortifying us for whatever encounters that may follow.

Street Dreams

At a recent St. Jerome's Home-School Association (I call it our Catholic PTA), two childhood friends, Gail Fletcher and Ann Marie Byrnes asked me: "Gootchie, why do you write about those other streets in the neighborhood?" –probably referring to the Morgan Street article. "Why dontcha write about Wallace, say, and Doro's where we used to hang out?" (It was across from the Healy School between 30th and 31st Street.)

I knew what my boosters meant, so I explained that I try to focus on what's of general interest in the area. Secretly, though, I do reminisce, but that's a double-edged sword.

My friends were hinting too at what we've all discovered; what makes wistful philosophers of us all. The sweet joys of our youth can never be recaptured, like grabbing at air. Live in the past, as good as anyone's memories are or certain times actually were, and you'll never be at ease in any present life. You could always make a good argument that "things aren't as good as they used to be", comparing a today with a yesterday.

And isn't that the dilemma, girls? Do modern times seem of little substance materially and spiritually (and I know I'm speaking in generalities). Or is it just that we are the grown-ups now, the new old-timers, to be disregarded as we respectfully (we always were respectful as teens even in our rebellious stages, or does time just make that seem so too?) assured our elders back then that we weren't immature as we listened to Valerie Carr play on Doro's jukebox: "Padre, Padre, what happened to our love so true?"

I thought of what you said, and after the meeting, I walked the neighborhood late at night. I stood for a while on the southeast corner of 31st and Wallace, and I stared across the intersection at the mailbox I used to sit on in front of the Modern Pharmacy when that was a hangout at one stage of my life. Before the drugstore's present aluminum and yellow brick façade, it had cast iron columns and tall panes of glass with hairpin and Coty and Kodak camera displays in the windows, and signs suggested you buy Sal Hepatica, Phillip's Tooth Powder or have film developed in only 7 days. Jerry Schwartz was the clerk we punk kids signified with as he made sundaes or phosphates for us at the marble ice cream fountain where the turnstile is now, inside the front door. Jerry is Doctor Schwartz now, and the Bridgeport Medical Center is his in the next block.

I looked across the street at the Bridgeport Funeral Home. In the late 40's, I played cowboys and Indians there in the vacant lot we called the prairie. With Mickey and Danny Sheehan in our make-believe Wild West. When they erected the concrete forms to build the foundations for a grocery store in the 50's, we scrambled up and down the excavations and toppled so much plywood that it looked like bombed-out Berlin after the war.

And when the grocery store was operating, I

needed a date for a De Paul Dance, and I decided to go at the proverbial last minute. At 6 p.m. on a busy Saturday, I asked Jackie Bonds, who was cashiering at the time. "—sure, Gootch, I'd love to," she surprised me. And I picked her up at her home in half an hour, both of us laughing all the way there how she got off of work. Now the site is a chapel, with more poignant meanings.

There's a story for every building, I thought, just as there's a story in each of you for every square inch of our neighborhood. If we keep writing down everything that we know from Pitney to 47th Street, Wentworth to Archer, maybe we'll get the whole story told and maybe figure out the meaning of it all, too.

Pumpkin Hunt Stirs Visions of Faded Days of Yesteryear
Chicago Sun Times , October 28 , 2010

It took my wife and me over two hours to escape the urban sprawl to find a farm stand in Anywhere, Illinois, for produce to put on our Bridgeport front porch for Halloween.

We exited near Huntley to Route 47, heading south, parallel to the city. The first and only sign we saw simply said "Pumpkins," and we drove west down a side road. After about a mile, and no such place, I suspected the sign had been left fading there from some yesteryear.

Then, just as suddenly, it came into view among the patch-quilt cornfields—a dirt drive lined with pumpkins and colored gourds and fall mums, leading us to a modest frame home.

The first sounds we heard were birds flitting in the trees; a hen and a rooster (for sale, for $6 each) cackling and crowing in small cages; goat's neahing, and the required dog barking the alarm. A young boy came out and just as shyly went back in—for, we later would learn, home-schooling—but not before he showed us the honor system pay box for our purchases.

The farmer came in from a field for a quick something. Answering my hurried questions (he said the family would be harvesting by flashlight that night before the first frost), he told me the barn was 100 years old and his ancestors had lived in the area since the 1830s.

I drove home reluctantly, filled with thoughts of an idyllic self-sufficient farm life (not considering the long workdays and risks), and I couldn't help but contrast it with the trucks lugging along on the Stevenson and the TV news helicopters overhead.

I thought of the quiet standing corn, and the shoulder-to-shoulder people in the Loop.

I thought of the honor system pay box, and the locked gates to our front and back yards.

I thought (sadly) of Carl Sandburg's lament, "Prairie Mother, I am one of your boys."

One of your lost boys.

Personal Column: LOST
A Bridgeport Neighborhood Restaurant

…last seen along 26th St., 31st, 43rd, Wallace, Halsted, Morgan and Archer: Picture-framed within a 25' wide cast-iron storefront. Wooden booths for maybe 20 people lined one wall, and stools for 10 more were at a sit-down counter on the opposite side. Owned by a neighborhood Greek or Italian.

The food was standard fare: Hamburgers that dripped off the cooking grease with the aroma of the meat it just fried; French fries made from fresh potatoes, and cokes that tasted more syrupy than just like carbonated water.

A jukebox was in the middle of the back wall with "Topsy, Part II", "To Know Him is to Love Him", "High School Confidential" and "Ain't That a Shame" on it.

Neighborhood teenagers were always permitted there—no imitation Fonzies of Pat Benatars, however: the real things. They knew who they were – they were destined to wear the original Levi's that felt like another layer of thick skin on their legs and high school or leather jackets with the collars turned up. They smoked—but not grass or pot. And they swore, too—but not in front of adults in public and especially not around younger children. They were frisky, wise-cracking, hand-holders: tough, soft, nervous, calm, pimple-faced, clear skinned, bold, shy, leaders, followers—but when told to "Keep it down," by the owner, they did.

Adults were also allowed in there. They were considered "out of it", but human beings, then. They used to sit more amused than irritated at that passing scene, knowing that their cuffed pants or the ladies' cloth coats weren't "Cool" looking. But the rock-and-rollers didn't realize as they watched those "old-timers" sip their coffee, that twenty years before them, they lived through an agonizing 1930s era and a frightful World War, and the James Dean look among the guys and the matching book-end look of the girls didn't intimidate them after what they'd been through.

"Characters" were often seen in and out of there: The Apple Annies; the Shopping Bag carriers with most of their life's possessions inside; troubled-looking souls with far-away looks; the would-be Marilyn Monroes whose real beauty sadly escaped them years before, with gaudy lipstick that overshot the mark; the genuinely poor and lonely-looking ones who you knew had nobody to attach to. Some mooched smokes, and others you gave money to without them even asking.

The Romova Grill was a definite stop at one time after patrons enjoyed a film at the Ramova Theater just down the street! The grill is still an intrinsic part of the neighborhood that hasn't lost its soul!.

Not a jukebox 'hangout' but one of the older beloved restaurants (since 1939) in Bridgeport with many similarities.

Wooden booths along one wall, a telephone booth yet on the back one, a sit-down counter, and the grills within eyesite where the owner-cook prepares your orders.

Well—I lost this place over twenty years ago, and I miss it at times, really. I don't know what kind of reward to offer you for finding it, but if you do, I'll at least take you there for a cup of coffee or a coke

By John Aranza 61

and some fries: and I'll even wear my old De La Salle jacket and be the butt of jokes as I unkindly made of others at times. And if it isn't everything that I said it was, I'll probably feel ashamed for bragging so; but deep down inside of me I know I'll be thinking that search through all of eternity, you'll never find another place that could make me feel different.

You go Home, Teresa, Everything Will Be All Right There

If there's anything in our 'big city' to compare with waking up in a small town in northwest Illinois, please point it out to me. I'm thinking of Galena and recalling the last time I was there. The stillness outside of the Grant Hills motel at seven in the morning.

The only sounds are from small birds chirping, whatever they quickly "chirp, chirp, chirp, chirp, chirp" to each other at the beginning of each day. And if there's any industrial sound, it's only and always a diesel somewhere, echoing like a trombone blast over the vacuum of the fields of crops and through the surrounding hills.

This came to mind while I was reading Bob Greene's column in Monday's Tribune. His story was a Teresa Iandola's, a DePaul Freshman from Pearl City, Illinois, population 550, titled: " 'L' Ride in the City a Far Cry From Home." That's what sent me to my car to examine my Illinois roadmap and determine what her neighborhood was like.

"In Pearl City," she told Greene, "our house doesn't even have a street number. We live on a rural route. I don't even carry a key in Pearl City. There's no reason to lock doors." Can you imagine her distress then—Greene sympathetically did—when her wallet was stolen out of her backpack at the 'L' stop. Her mother sent her money to buy a new wallet, and she did. And that was stolen, along with her glasses, for a second time in a week, again when she was on the 'L' platform.

She said that the police that assisted her couldn't have been nicer, and they told how bad they felt for her, but also "...that this was Chicago, and I had to learn a different way to behave. They said I

couldn't go around trusting people. They said I had to be looking out for myself at every moment, or I'd be in trouble." "I'm trying to learn to be careful," she said, "I'm trying to remember not to be too friendly to other people. I know that it's best to be very paranoid now. When I walk up the stairs I look around me. I never was like that before, but now I have to be." She said that she didn't like being this way. "I was raised to think that if you acted in a good way toward others, then your niceness would come back to you. Now I'm learning that's not how life is." Greene wrote that she wants to stay in Chicago and in school, but something inside her tells her she doesn't really belong here.

"I think it would help me a lot if I could go back to Pearl City for just a little while," she said. "I'd like to sort of recharge there. Just sit around home and think about things. I don't feel very good these days."
You'll come to conclusions about her situation; I am sure, just as I have with my own.

Her story makes me think of how enormous and unwieldy a city our size is, of course, preventing us from knowing 3,000,000 people, welcoming our visitors or being able to shake the person who did this and say: "Hey, what' ya think you're doin'?"

It makes me think of the meaningless repetition of how many television police shows, had the producers, actors, or sponsors suffered the fear of this girl, they'd be ashamed of their existence.

And it makes me think of small-town girl whose words seemed calloused—and why, why I keep thinking, why must it happen to any of the young?—into a new philosophy.

You go home for a while, Teresa, like you said. It's not an escape, but it'll probably make you feel better to hear the sound of an old tractor and not the impersonal rattle of an elevated car, carrying, perhaps, how many other calloused hearts?

And recharge, as you said that you wanted to. But don't stop acting in a good way towards others until that niceness comes back to you. Maybe your 'niceness' that comes through in Greene's column has changed the thinking of some person among us, and what would life be like if there weren't persons like you?

The Long Season

Finally its over. The MBA has ended for another summer. (The Monday Night Basketball Association).

What began as a gym class for me and my childhood boyfriends at the Salvation Army as the Red Devils in the early 50's, has continued yearly each fall to spring as our weekly basketball night and workout.

Some took early retirements: Dan Sheehan, Maurice Sullivan and Jack Isaacson, and some went down with injury as Bruce Alphin did this year, perhaps ending a career that spanned five decades, though he's consulting with team physician Dr. Basil Rathbone about a bionic knee.

For those of us who complete this at times exhausting ordeal, we say Thank You to our wives and children. It wasn't easy.

Oh, many of you have Bingo and bowling and golf and bunco and wagering, but our compulsion takes us on the Road (Archer, Pulaski or Ashland on our ways to the gym we used at Davis Square Park), and then many times afterwards on a Long Night's Journey Into Days as we unwound at Kairis' at 33rd and Union, often thinking about our wives when it was time to go home.

Much to the The Wagon restaurant's growing concern, we recently had what we call our annual Awards Banquet there. (No one would praise us for what we do, so we compliment ourselves.) Ed Walz and Jim Marzano our exemplary Commissioner and Treasurer who both had the only perfect attendance for the season, awarded the trophies appropriately titled, genuinely earned and mostly dubious honors to receive.

Bob Green won the Contact Award, not referring to what you'll read later, but because he plays basketball like the player he must have been when he was the MVP on De La Salle's 1970 football team.

His cousin, Bill Green, won the Bernard Johnson Award. For those of you not familiar with the refinements of the game, 'that's the equivelant of getting the job done like those ladies who attend the annual mark-down sale at New York city's Macy's or Gimbels; when the doors open, get our of the way or don't pick up the goods (the ball) they (he's) after.

The Balich's, our younger progeny, Tom, Chris and Johnny (Age first; Where is Their Beauty?) won the Hanson Brother's Award, based on the movie "Slapshot." Their cousin, John Peso, probably won the only sincere award for his all-around good play.

Ken Kolerich was characteristically silent through all of this until I threw a ceremonious wine glass past him off of the back all after we all sang "Zivila", a Croatian drinking song, like Mario Lanz toasting "Drink, Drink, Drink," in the "Student Prince."

"I'm getting out of here," Kenny awoke.

Well, we did pay our bill and tip generously, What's the rush? The night is young.

At our sponsor afterwards, Ted Rewers' Kairis Corner, we said our last farewells before our trips home.

War is Hell. Who Said Life is Easy? Men Without Women. All of the old adages are true.

After a few drinks, we sighed a collective relief off of the grueling year.

But Gigi becoming the beauty that she was, Bob Green put a flower over his ear from a bouquet on a table, and "he wasn't that funny, awkward girl we knew."

When does warmth become desire? Suddenly he was waltzing in our arms, First mine, though I had to remind him to keep his hands on my shoulders. Marzano anxiously cut in, then so did Bruce and Billy.

Later, Bobby played some Country and Western song about "Jose Cuervo, " I think it went, "-you are a friend of mine." And some of the love-starved sickies did a barn dance type reel, hooking one certain customer a if he were in a revolving door each time he tried to go to the washroom.

Ted, our friend and benefactor, was on our side of the bar for the first time because he had just sold the

By John Aranza 63

tavern that week. But he almost sent the new owner's customers home at 10 after 12, mistaking it for 2:00 when he began shutting off the neon lights in the front window.

Me? I thought I was Elvis on a pool stick to Chuck Berry's "Johnny B. Goode." Bill Green kept saying "You only go around once in life." So we all were records on a turntable. He did manage to soothe the restive herd for a while when he sang the haunting "Danny Boy."

But all right. O,K. I'll try once more next year guys, knowing what it means to be on the Road again, separated from those we love that one night a week, or is it longing to be separated?

Please don't confuse me?; just let me finish this song?

O Gigi...
When did your sparkle
turn to fire?

Oh what Miracle has made
you the way you are?"

I'd prefer not to have this article signed, but if the Editor insists in truth and full disclosure, I'm John Aranza

Bridgeport Family Medical center S.C.
Quality Healthcare The Way It Was Meant To Be

3201 S. Wallace St
Chicago, IL 60616

Dr. Jerrold Schwartz
Dr. Peter J. Reed
Dr. Deanna Placko PA.C.

Phone: (312) 326-3200
Fax: (312) 326-3207

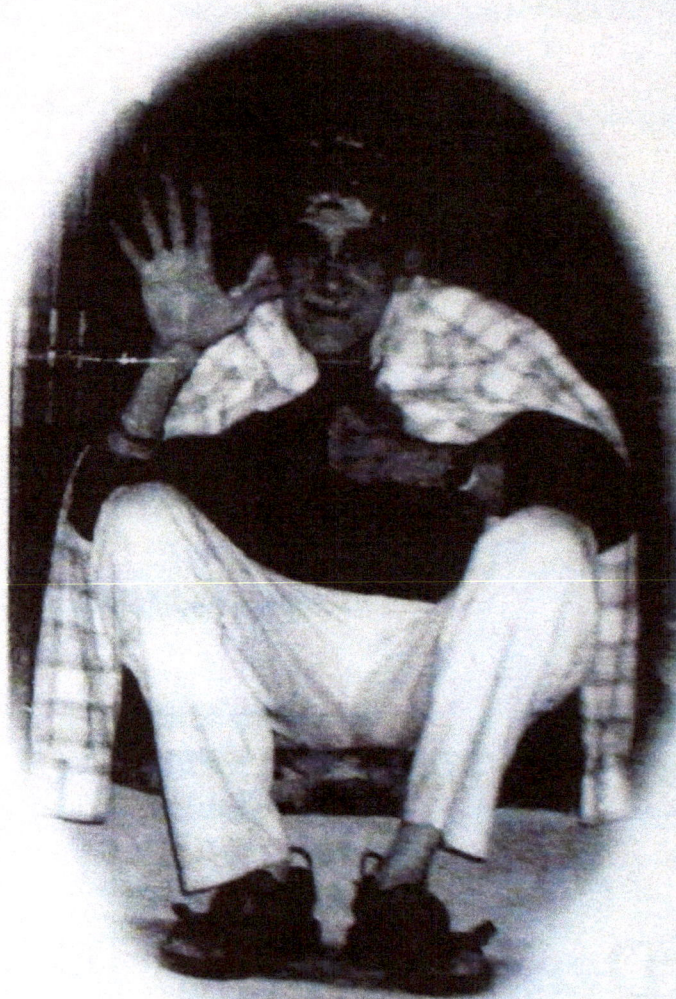

Mass of Resurrection
In Honor of

Ray Biamonte

Born into Eternity January 14, 2004

An excerpt by the Biamonte family , from an otherwise unrelated article , for the Memorial Mass pamphlet of a beloved , life-long Armour Square resident

"And when I passed 31st and Princeton, Ray Biamonte, single, just another one of us who lives among the two-flats and bungalows, was watching the parade for his friends who were in it.

And I thought back to when his mother was alive, and the first and only time I met her was when he pushed her in a wheelchair to Armour Park and he lifted her in his arms and placed her on a blanket under a tree to have her refreshed in the outdoor air. And he said: 'John, I want you to meet my Mom.'

And this is what we're about in this neighborhood too, I thought.

Publicized or not. Seeking recognition or not. Living out our lives as best we can, and being most times only what we know ourselves to be."

— John Aranza,
Bridgeport News, August 22, 1984

Come to the Neighborhood

In the Chicago Catholic recently, I read of the Archdiocese's plan for Englewood : consolidation of the parishes, resulting in three school closings . Last Wednesday's Chicago Tribune reported it too: "The Catholic Archdiocese of Chicago, battered by dramatic population shifts and burdened by aging and outsized school buildings in some areas. has begun an unprecedented and controversial reorganization in a number of neighborhoods." Avoiding a back-up on the Ryan Friday, I exited on 67th for quicker side streets and happened to pass one of those parishes. St. Bernards, occupying half a city block between Stewart and Harvard at 66th Street. Still-inspiring yellow brick structrures, built perhaps in the Teens or 20's; one, undoubtedly, a four-story high school once, now a public adult education center; a grammar school, church, parish center and a Spanish-tiled roofed convent or rectory. I'm an old Catholic boy, and I could tell that this abundant construction and present good maintainence refelcted years of original and presently concerned parishioners. But surrounded by what? Gap-toothed blocks of vacant lots and Victorian homes, some with boards ready to fall , hanging loosely off the porches. Garages-once carriage houses with servant's quarters above- like hundred year old barns I've seen on rides in the country, ready to collapse.

Then periodically. proud owners' homes with aluminum siding showing their wanting to improve . As I turned west onto 63rd Street and into a corridor of new townhomes that shielded those blocks behind, as our Loop skyline doesn't portray all that the city is beyond either, I thought of the help that area cried out for: the frustrations the Trib and Catholic reported of the parishoners affected: the total planning needed; how those barren lots and forlorn-looking buildings

Some neighborhood ethnic groups took a final picture with a loved one outside of a church , funeral chapel or at the gravesite . Here , relatives , neighbors and friends gather around the deceased in this undated photo , appearing to be in the 1920`s  ,  in front of Saint George`s

might be said could reflect the barren ideas of whom? Allowing this decay to become so pervading.

In those same articles, mention was also made of the consolidation study currently being made for our Bridgeport parishes, St. David's, Nativity, St. George's. All Saints-St. Anthony's, among others, and I wondered how the silent ways of change - like a person not knowing they've aged, until an unmistakeable feature suddenly appears in a mirror one day - are affecting us here in the neighborhood?

And it isn't a 'Catholic' or a 'religious ' problem alone. It's a cultural one; a social one; a part of your body you could loose, but never be the same without. If Doremus Congregational Church or the Salvation Army on 31st and Normal, or the First Lutheran Church of the Trinity at 31st and Lowe, or the Valentine Boy's Club on Emerald. the Benton House on Gratten, or St.

Mary of Perpetual Help or St. Barbara's High Schools were to close each would represent a far greater loss than their evident importance: a loss of their need: the ability of the people to support it: or of the enrichment they provide for the neighborhood, just as that St. Bernard's must. If an eloquent John F. Kennedy was among the City Council instead of the Tower of Babel sounds we seem to hear, he would surely say : "Let them go to Englewood; let them come to Bridgeport," caring for the plight he'd see there, heeding the warning signs he'd see here. Or am I only imagining what isn't here? fantacizing on a notion after a chance drive through a nearby eloquent community'?

Are we secure in what we take for granted around us sometimes? Or should we all be doing something more to maintain every vital organ of our person we call the   neighborhood'?

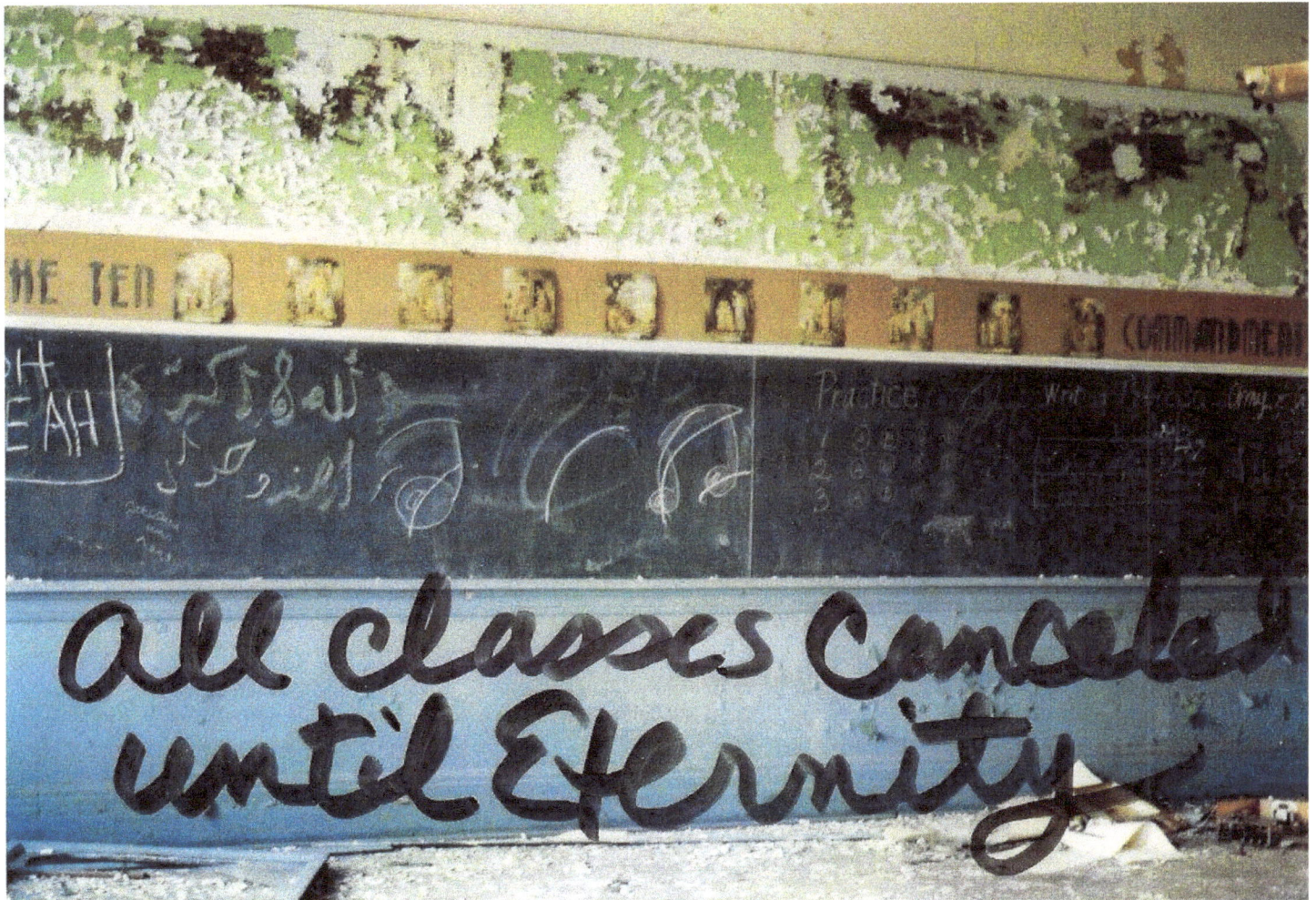

Abandoned St Bridget's Classroom

By John Aranza 69

Our fears were realized as neighborhood churches were merged, closed, changed - demolished.

There will be no masses today...

... and ever again . 1992   (Saint Bridgets was the first Southside Catholic Parish , originally a Mission of Saint Patrick`s. In Europe , churches are preserved for over a thousand years . Here , some for less than a hundred .

The unsubstantiated rumor in Chicago always was that one person moved the Stevenson Expressway around to the back of Saint Bridget`s to prevent its destruction in the early 1960`s . Superman ? Paul Bunyon ? Who else could be so powerful ? Anyway , that was probably welcomed by a couple named Richard J. Daley and Eleanor Guilfoyle who were married there in 1936 . And in another union   - this one of Technology and the Celestial - I can attest to hearing Citizen`s Band interference intermittantly in the P.A. system during Mass,   of truckers communcating with each other from the roadway which was within yards of the church .

St. Barbara school to shut after 76 years

BY BRENDA WARNER ROTZOLL
STAFF REPORTER

St. Barbara High School in Bridgeport, founded 76 years ago to serve Polish immigrants, will close June 1 because the all-girls school has just 85 students left.

The closing was announced Friday by the Rev. Michael T. Yakaitis, pastor of the St. Barbara parish, and the school principal, Dorene A. Hurckes.

Students wept and worried about their futures but were assured the school would help place those not graduating this year in nearby Catholic high schools, Hurckes said.

She said Maria, Lourdes, Our Lady of Tepeyac and Holy Trinity high schools have indicated they have room for the St. Barbara students, and for the 12 teachers, as well.

"The tradition of attending a neighborhood parish high school has long since been replaced by shopping around, considering a myriad of choices," Yakaitis said.

St. Barbara was founded in 1925 as a two-year commercial high school for girls and boys. Then, and for many years, it was staffed by the Sisters of St. Joseph, Third Order of St. Francis. In 1947, it became a four-year comprehensive school for girls. Enrollment peaked in 1985 at 372 students, then began a steady decline.

Last-ditch measures failed to draw more students. Every classroom was wired for computers. Distance learning was added for the college prep track. And for the girls planning to go straight to work after high school, the latest computer technology was taught.

Yakaitis said there are too few students left for tuition and gifts to support the school. Under archdiocese rules, parish-sponsored schools may not receive direct financial aid from the parish.

Lately, half of St. Barbara students have come from the Chicago Public Schools. No longer mostly of Polish extraction, the student body is 51 percent white, 39 percent Hispanic, 5 percent African American and 4 percent Asian.

There are 267 elementary and 45 high schools in the Archdiocese of Chicago, which includes Lake and Cook counties.

The archdiocese has said any further closings this year will be announced March 31.

By John Aranza 71

Doremus Congregational Church, now

newlife *Community Church*

St. George Baptismal Font
and Paschal Candle
Beginning and end

Once again, the parishes of the Bridgeport area, along with the Chicago Archdiocese, faced a major problem. The people of the area could no longer support so many parishes. Therefore, after many long hours of painful meetings, decisions were made and overturned. In April of 1990, the Parishioners of Saint George Parish were told of the Archdiocese's decision to close its doors. The final Celebration of the Eucharist was held on Saturday, June 30, 1990. The main Celebrant was Father Richard Dodaro and many past associates and friends.

Although Saint George will cease to exist as a parish, it will always exist in our hearts and minds. The memories will continue. The things we, as a Family, cherish most will continue to be admired by a new Family. With the help of Fr. Dodaro and Fr. Saulaitis, and with the consent of the Archdiocese, many of our church's contents will be sent to Lithuania. They are destined for Blessed George Matulaitis Parish near Vilnus. May it help them serve God as it has helped us.

May the new Family
enjoy this Window
as much as the past
Family.

AND OUR END..........

The Other Side of the Moon

Last week I wrote that a Sun-Times reporter wanted to contact me about writing a feature story about Bridgeport.

The election was behind is, I thought. We could finally let Chicago know what else we were about: Our little ethnic shops and quaint streets. The artists among us. Our heritage. The I & M Canal beginning here. We the people. The city in microcosm. How disappointingly wrong I was.

I left my telephone number for her to call me at home, but she didn't. And when I called her this past Monday at the newspaper, she said she was already completing the article for this coming Friday's edition: On Racism in Bridgeport.

I didn't want to respond to this in our paper, but isn't it time for us to say, "Stop this baiting and antagonizing of our neighborhood and the city?" I was so disgusted to hear Barbara Shullgasser and her predetermined notions that I couldn't complete the story I had begun for today.

Here was a New Yorker, only a six-year resident of Chicago, saying she wanted to write about the attitudes everyone knows about.

"Knows about?" I replied indignantly—"what everyone looks for. Even Jesus Christ lost his temper chasing the money changers out of the Temple," I said, "if that's what you want to focus on." She said, "No," that she didn't visit our churches. "No" she didn't explore the Polish, Lithuanian, Irish, Italian, and other neighborhoods within the neighborhood. "Yes," she did read my article last week on one representative family, but it didn't even elicit a reply from when I said that's what our community is all about.

"Everybody has a dark side of their nature—if that's what you want to look for," I continued. "Why don't you write about the sensibilities of our community?" I asked.

"Why don't you write about what unites us rather than be so divisive?" I persisted.

I'm going to save any further comments until after Friday's edition of the Sun-Times comes out.
There is a saying in Croatian:
"The earth swore to
the Heavens that every
minute little thing
will be known."

All I hope is that the reason for such malicious contempt becomes known, and that the goodness that is in all of us will be the only criteria that will identify us as a neighborhood and continually guide our actions.

By John Aranza 73

Knock On Any Door
"...down this street."

I thought of the foreward in Willard Motley's dramatic Chicago novel, not thinking of the tragic Nick Romano, but saying it because it rolled so easily off my tongue, so lyrically, and so appropriately. I thought, when I walked down Morgan Street and reflected on what it means to our neighborhood.

Morgan Street?

I know what some of you are thinking: What's he doing on Morgan?

If you were raised East of Halsted as I was, it was as far away from your thoughts as if it didn't even exist. And if you walk its blocks today from 31st to 33rd distracted by what isn't there, the life gone out of it (the department stores and bank, newspaper and jewelers, and doctors and dentists and bakeries) whose windows to the world were inharmoniously sealed forever in "modern" converted fronts of perma-stone, siding, common brick or glassblocks, you may miss those who survive, the proud ones who remain (unheralded as we all somehow feel and are in our day-to-day lives) and the fact that nowhere in Bridgeport has any block or neighborhood within it so vividly conveyed the feeling of a little village to itself, an "Our Town, " a world of its own, as this one did.

Look high up the walls of the many buildings with names and dates as testimonials, "Piotrowski," "Czechowicz," "Jakubaitis," "1912," below the ornate rooflines. Absorb the classical architecture such as the decorative festoons in the lintels above the 2nd floor windows at 3235 or the urns atop the parapet of the building two doors south. Discover the abundant facades that are completed in scallop or steppe-design as they reach the peak, some with limestone or metal finials, and all reminiscent of the great cities of Europe. Of course, a wellspring of human activity didn't create this with the knowledge that it would be praised generations later.

But you who live there sensed this, just as Harriet Lescauskas has observed it since 1934 when she began operating the pharmacy in her family's building at 3337 S. Morgan.

(I didn't tell her once during my visit there that the older oak display cases and back counters; the plants in the front window appreciatively facing the warm sustenance of the afternoon sun; and the absence of pop and milk coolers and cameras and wrist watches and clothes, was comforting in a dignified way that you didn't need a hard sell to be sold on something.)

Harriet isn't forceful either, yet just as convincing in the gentle, unpretentious way of her existence. Her father came to Morgan Street from Lithuania in 1899, "When there were mostly cabbage fields here," he told her. And she explained that's why some built their homes at the back of the lots (as at 3344) to keep up the old-country ways of farms and gardens, then prominently facing the street.

But everything she told me of Morgan Street seemed to confirm the cohesiveness of the early lives of these people, many of whom worked in the stockyards as her father had. She explained that Morgan Street was a gateway into the Stockyards, and it achieved its prominence before the useage of Halsted Street as we know it today.

"First I remember there being no cars. My parents even packed lunches to go to funerals. They were taken in horsedrawn coaches to the far-out cemeteries, and they wouldn't return until the evening. Then we had street cars."

When I asked her about the other businesses on the street, she knew their names and locations as if they had closed only recently: "Kuchinskas had a bakery at 34th and Morgan, and after the father died, about 40 years ago, the boys changed their names to Kuchun, and the business too. Now they own the Holsum Bread Co."

I looked out of her front window again. There were only school children outside, playing their way home from the P.D. Armour School around the corner. Across the street, the old Eagle Show was an auto repair shop, and the ice cream parlor next to it at 3322 closed for twenty years. "-what was in the 50' wide building at 3318 next to it, where apartments were made out of stores?" I asked.

Who could tell that the next arched entrance way once led into a church? She said that her father told her the building was moved to that site from somewhere else. At different times afterwards, there was a jewelry store, a tailor shop and a tavern where ladies couldn't pass the curtain inside the front entrance, and people brought home .5 cent pails of beer. In the back, there was a Turkish steam bath where you patted yourself with dried out oak leaves, "- but I couldn't tell you the medicinal benefit of that," she laughed.

Two doors north at 3312 is most of the neighborhoods memory of Morgan Street: The New National Ballroom. The Bucket of Blood. (Whose reputation was greater than the fraternal and social groups who own the building and still meet upstairs.) "We had a doctor in our building, Dr. Weiner and he would treat people injured in the fights that carried into the street from the doings inside, until we simply had to close our doors at night."

Morgan Street also had a Tananevicz Bank (now the vacant NE corner at 33rd) and the Katalikas Newspaper printed in the loft building next to it with its name still on the cornice stone, and distributed nationally from the building across the street at 3244. Where the Weller Department Store name is on the torn awning at 3219, Budricks and Struzynski also had department stores where the clerks put money into wire baskets that were sent on a trolley to the cashier on the mezzanine level in the back.

I asked her about the Lithuanians and the Poles living so close together, thinking of each of their neighborhoods and St. George's Parish a block East on Lituanica and St. Mary of Perpetual Help and Immaculate Conception to the west of Morgan. "Oh, there were 'disagreements' about 'whose' street it was," and we both smiled knowingly, since most of Bridgeport has mellowed and melted into the more harmonious family that we have now.

Leaving her store I thought that only having a neighborhood cemetery somewhere nearby prevented them from having that complete village of their own, just as all-encompassing as my father's birthplace in Yugoslavia, where my cousins walked me to the church where he was an altar boy and to the graveyard where our ancestors are buried.

But Morgan Street's vitality isn't all in the past. It still offers some of Bridgeport's oldest and well-known traditions: Paul Studio, Pulaski Savings,

Bridgeport Quality Market and Morgan Paint, among others. And the newly-formed Morgan Street Council is achieving the rights and quiet enjoyment that neighborhood deserves. I think our late Mayor Daley would have recognized this need too and would have felt that what was good for Morgan Street was good for Bridgeport.

Where do we go from here? New ways of life are constantly, if not sublty, altering the old. Will it ever be resolved what is better : What used to be? and what is now?

Me? I'll probably view what was as "touchstones" of what family, neighborhood, pride and culture should be, but wondering too if Pac Man and Video Parlors and jean stores will be the future traditions of the eclectic outpourings we have created, and I know you'll endlessly discuss this too.

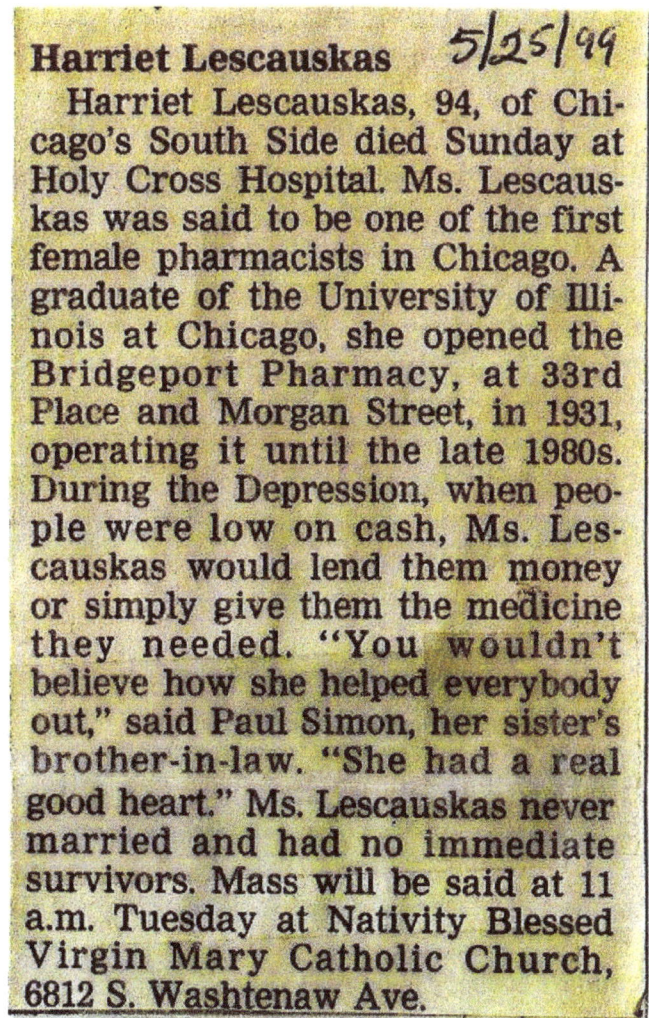

Harriet Lescauskas 5/25/99

Harriet Lescauskas, 94, of Chicago's South Side died Sunday at Holy Cross Hospital. Ms. Lescauskas was said to be one of the first female pharmacists in Chicago. A graduate of the University of Illinois at Chicago, she opened the Bridgeport Pharmacy, at 33rd Place and Morgan Street, in 1931, operating it until the late 1980s. During the Depression, when people were low on cash, Ms. Lescauskas would lend them money or simply give them the medicine they needed. "You wouldn't believe how she helped everybody out," said Paul Simon, her sister's brother-in-law. "She had a real good heart." Ms. Lescauskas never married and had no immediate survivors. Mass will be said at 11 a.m. Tuesday at Nativity Blessed Virgin Mary Catholic Church, 6812 S. Washtenaw Ave.

"Whad'ya Say Be Bop?"

This article is about nicknames. A fawning parent; a character trait; a real first name you wanted to hide; your boyfriends, girlfriends, or schoolmate—all these were the sources of those tags we wear like status symbols in Bridgeport, or maybe flinch when someone meets us on 31st Street and calls out in front of strangers: B.A. (Ken Kolerich)—you still playing basketball?"

I haven't asked one person for information in writing this; I wanted it to be spontaneous. I'm sure that you could do as I did and recall any number of names from your experience. Here goes, and there's no protecting the innocent.

In '57, Be Bop (Ray Beckman) hung around with the group I was in at 30th and Union—Weasel, Flash, Hans, Minnow, Boris, Sol, and Beans. Oh, I'm sorry; they were Ed Weingartner, Frank La Barbera, Berry McMeel, Bernard Ernst, James Scialabba, Maurice Sullivan, and Dan Sheehan, among others.

Go ahead. Laugh. I hear some of you—but don't let any of us find out if you're hiding some nickname you hope never sees the light of day again.

Even before then, there were so many other acquaintances from my St. Anthony De Padua parish or nearby St. John's or from the parks with names like charms on a key chain: Two of the McCarthy brothers were Rocket and Guts. There was Dago Joe (Amato) and the Greek (Tom Notides) and how many simply called Moje? Red? –Red Sheehan, Red Adamo, and Red Kuzmanich. Or how would you like to be called Garbage? (But it was respectful.)

Sis'es? Sis Chodor (Pavela), Sis Catura (Cozzi), and Sis Norton—and a Bro, too. (He'll forgive me for not knowing his real name. Don't you still know some people by their nicknames only?) He palled with my next-door neighbor, Nick Spata, at 3025 S. Parnell. My life-long friend Little Eddy (Walz) and I would watch in amazement when we were small as Bro would sit on the curb in front of Otto Richter's candy store in the middle of the block after playing a softball game in Healy Schoolyard. And he'd roll up his pants' cuffs and wipe the dust off his wooden leg, and then begin polishing it.

There's Doc McCarry, and Midge Alyinovich (and his brother Kick). And Whitey Miller and Whitey Gelbuda, and Satch Dooner, Pinball, Squash, Cheetah, Hunk, Canal St., Brain, Midnight, Greensleeves and what's that? Some of you are saying that John can dish it out, but he can't take it?

All right, I'll tell you my nickname. It's Gootchie. (Keep laughing, but don't forget what I said before.) One time I called Fred Frugoli, and his wife Arlene answered the phone. I asked her to get her husband, simply referring to all of our nicknames: "Cookie. Tell Butch that Gootchie's on the phone."
I guess it's human nature to call most people by a name that's a form of endearment, so we have a Richie, now, in an esteemed position, and there was an Ike and a Harry at one time. That's not bad company to be in, is it?

Well, I have to go now. Baba (that's my mother. It's pronounced Bub-uh, phonetically, meaning grandmother, in Croatian.) said that my sister Tootsie (Phyllis) came to see me. Please finish this? And insert the nicknames used within your families or group of friends.

And excuse me, while I turn up this old radio and hear the ending of Jimmy Bowen's song:

"—listen, why-eye I say, Be Bop,
Love you Baby.
Be Bop, don't mean, maybe,
Be Bop, luh-uv you Baby.
I'm stick'n with you,
I'm stick'n with you."

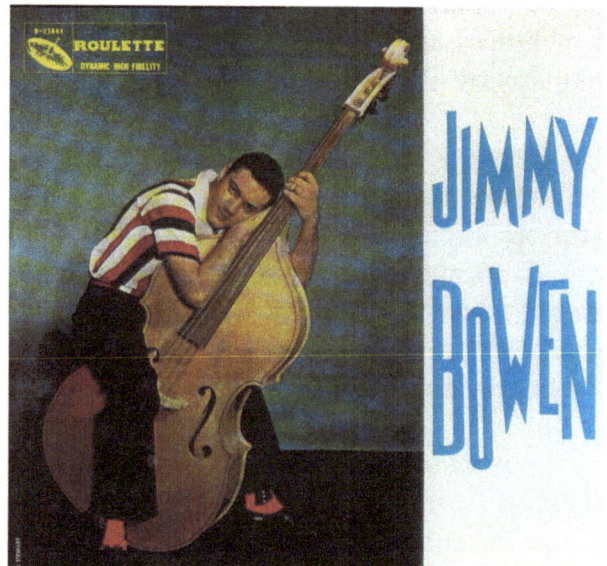

Reminiscing

Knetl's fostered Bridgeport's neighborhood shopping tradition

By John E. Aranza

Factories that are residential lofts now, on 35th Street near Morgan Street. Two-flats gutted and converted into single-family houses. Theatres closed and torn down. Parochial schools consolidated, their churches demolished. Stores with different uses, many now apartments with residential fronts. Time and change inexorably moving through the Bridgeport neighborhood.

Though many traditions remain, newcomers to the neighborhood may pass the Chinese restaurant at 31st St. and Wallace Ave. and never know about Tom Dimas's wonderful Quality Diner that was there before.

Passing 522 W. 32nd St., how could new area residents know that the modernized storefront building now for sale as a house for years had an awning above the now-removed plate glass windows

A dumpster is filled with the debris of the old Knetl's during the building's recent remodeling.

that read "Knetl's Food and Grocery?"

Today's traditions are formed in Jewel and Dominick's parking lots and wide-aisled stores. Bridgeport's traditions started in many of the mom-and-pop businesses. Dimas's Kopper Kettle, then the Quality Diner. Josie's

White Horse Restaurant. Knetl's.

"Dad bought his building and grocery in 1940 from his parents, and we lived in the back," Louise Knetl recalled. Louise and her sister, Joanne, recently sold the family property in favor of a traditional bungalow nearby.

In its heyday, "the grocery had

sawdust on the floors, and big barrels with pickles that you reached into to make your purchase," Louise fondly recalled. It also had "a Coca-Cola box with ice in which the bottles were kept, with an opener on the side."

There was an ice box that customers looked into to choose lunchmeats that the elder Knetl had prepared using a slicing machine. Bottles of milk kept there were delivered by Herb Martin from 30th and Normal Streets, who worked for the Betz Dairy on 33rd Street between Union and Lowe Streets.

"And some people would return the milk after removing the cap and taking off the cream on top, saying that the milk was spoiled," recalled Joanne, not too fondly.

"But dad was a very good man. Many people were 'on the cuff,' meaning they would owe for their purchases that were written down in a notebook. And people would pay a couple dollars a week or all at once—or not at all," said Joanne, and the sisters smiled

August 6, 2004

Gazette • 53

knowingly together.

The shelves were lined with Oxydol, Ivory Flakes, Big Jack soaps, and Log Cabin syrup tins. "Wish we had them now," said Joanne.

"There were cookies in open half-crates that Mom filled bags from and brought them to the counter," Joanne recalled. "And a metal Fusano Pie stand with pies in the shelves."

"We had some penny candy—licorice and dots on a paper strip," Louise said. "I'd get scolded for taking a handful and sharing with our friends, because I thought it was ours and I could give it away."

Joanne laughed and recalled how she would swing on a knotted rope from the back of a produce delivery truck right into the store, and then she would help unload it. She also delivered ten-cent newspapers to select customers nearby.

"Dad advertised vegetable specials with a Bon Ami [cleanser] paste written on the windows," Joanne said. "At Christmas, Arty across the street would help Mom create a Christmas scene of a little village made up of heavy cardboard buildings inside the front windows."

"And he taught me how to tie my shoelaces," Joanne added.

A National food chain store and a Del Farm on 31st Street a block away doomed Knetl's and Ahionovich's two blocks away on

Marie Knetl, Joseph Knetl Jr., and Joseph Knetl in their store loaded with anything a shopper could want in the 1930s.

30th Street, another store that served people "on the cuff." The chain stores put other local merchants out of business as well.

"We'd see people returning from shopping at a chain store with their bags, but they'd come back 'on the cuff' for small purchases like two slices of cheese that they couldn't buy there," Joanne recalled.

Would one ever even think of asking a cashier at a store now if one could come back and pay later?

Many are buying into Bridgeport now because it is a "hot" area close to downtown. This demand for housing is driving up prices to Near North Side levels.

One thing that money cannot

buy, however is the communal values accrued over time by people named Knetl and others like them.

Search the neighborhood for its traditions and its family values. Seek them out. Nurture them. Then, the neighborhood will continue to be the community it always was.

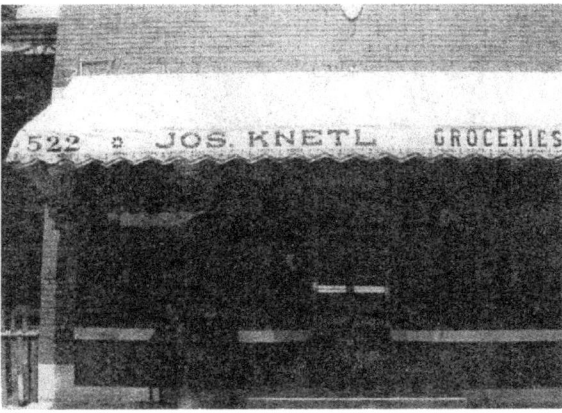

Wings on Halsted St…

In our everyday Bridgeport lives, we sometimes hardly notice the changes in our neighborhood that benchmark the passing of one generation to another; of the 30's to the war-era 40's; or the 60's into the 70's; even of a 1920's-styled storefront instantly "modernized into the present.

They occur subtly, and one day we realize that the Wallace Show is no longer that but a Bicycle Shop; that Harold and Alice Brady's 31st Street candy store had been closed and converted into an apartment, and well, come with me to Halsted Street, and we'll relive an event that shocked the world in 1933—the tragic flight of Captain Stefan Darius and Lieutenant Stanley Girenas—whose hectic preparations also brought them to the Jucus Sisters Restaurant in our community.

Lindberg pioneered non-stop flights across the Atlantic in 1927, and 29 others died before them trying to imitate Lindy. In 1933 America, passenger flights, if any, were made by twin-engine propeller planes that carried only 20 people. Mail flights to Europe didn't even begin until 1935. So a fete such as crossing the Atlantic was a brave accomplishment—attention getter. (Amelia Earhart was killed in the Atlantic in 1937, trying to be the first woman to fly solo across it.)

Darius' and Girenas' aim was not self-serving, either. Already distinguished in our military, they were flying enthusiasts and patriots whose sole purpose was to bring honor to their birthplace, Lithuania.

It was difficult to raise funds in the Depression, and they were helped by concerts, programs, and banquets.

They also gave flying lessons at Ashburn, Chicago's first airfield at 83rd Street, between Kostner and Cicero. An anxious student secretly took up their plane—and crashed—further complicating their plans. Needing a place to work, they repaired an engine in the basement of a relative's Jucus Sisters Restaurant at 3241-43 South Halsted Street.

Let's drive there. I'll park here, in front of the former Lithuania show. You don't recognize it? (All right, another time we'll talk about the "The Lost Theatres of Bridgeport".) We'll go to the corner and stand next to the old Universal State Bank, where Bunny Chevrolet used to have their Display Room. I know, it's a resale shop now, but 30's autos were shown right here in the window. There's the former restaurant building across the street; it's generally forgotten, as the work of those fliers within.

After taking off from New York on July 15, 1933, they flew 4,500 miles with a compass, the stars, courage and little else to guide them. They couldn't afford the further necessity of a radio and with their gasoline supply gone; they crashed and were killed less than 300 miles from Kaunas goal. They're proudly but sadly remembered by their Lithuanian friends. Auburn Street was changed to Lituanica, the name of their single-engine airplane. And the American Legion Post 44th and Western and the memorial at the entrance to Marquette Park testifies to them.

The Jucus Sisters Restaurant? It's Tony's Super Food Mart now. We can go in. You won't hear the drone of an airplane or the clinkling of dishes or the low murmur of talk in wooden booths. Only the metal sounds of shopping carts in the clean aisles of his food store. The ceramic floor and the glazed-tile sidewalks and ceilings were the most expensive items when the building was erected in the 20's. And at the base of the vegetable bins—you can see where a sit-down counter and stools lined the north wall. In the next room, they also had a Bakery and Meat Market. Of course, it's all changed.

Like an old snapshot with doily-like edges, that's what used to be. But you're being entertained with the fanciful images of the interestingly-lived past our Bridgeport can provide.

Welcome, voyager.

By John Aranza 79

S. L. FABIONAS CO'S.

BANQUET HELD ON DECEMBER 30, 1923, AT JUCUS RESTAURANT

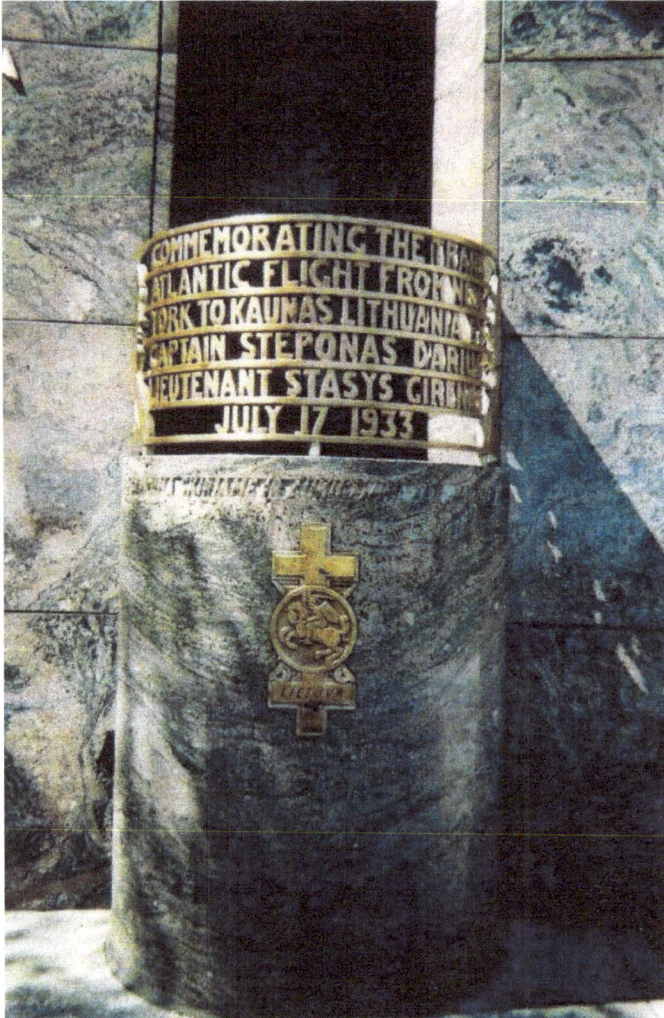

COMMEMORATING THE TRANS
ATLANTIC FLIGHT FROM NEW
YORK TO KAUNAS LITHUANIA
CAPTAIN STEPONAS DARIUS
LIEUTENANT STASYS GIRENAS
JULY 17 1933

Darius - Girenas monument in Marquette Park.

Stearns Quarry before Palmisano Park

George Bozinovich, Nearing 100

When I asked George what was the happiest thing he could recall in his life, he let his head rest on the back of the chair and he closed his eyes, expressioning: What happiness?

His son, Peter, sitting across from me in his dad's parlor mirrored his father's thoughts, as he had so remarkably throughout this visit: "Work. Pa's always worked."

"My Johnny. You can't be (happy). It's always work—or no bread," he began in his Croatian accent. "C'mon. C'mon—the foreman would always call us by our names. Hurry up, he'd push everyone."

"Us"? Hod carriers and laborers as he had been when he came from Sinj, Yugoslavia in 1910.

"I work first on buildings then car lines for .15 cents an hour," he knew with exact recall. "I came to America to lose my life," he thought when he worked with a pick in a snow-filled, cold trenches his first winter here.

He came to America for a "better" life, as millions of Europeans had. The last survivor of 21 children, he was born on a farm.

"Were there hospitals?" I asked foolishly.

"Johnny, if you needed a Doctor, it would take 2 days for someone to go and bring him back. I was born by Babica (midwife); all of us were."

Suddenly, the span of his life overwhelmed me. April 12, 1884. George was born about 20 years after the Civil War and Lincoln. There were no telephones. No airplanes in the entire world. No automobiles being produced. Queen Victoria ruled England.

"What was home like?" I asked.

"A stone farm building. We burn wood on clay in center of floor," he gestured to the rug. "Above, no ceiling, only floor beams. So fire heat us, and smoke rising cured pork and beef hanging there. My mother cook over fire too, by lifting and lowering pots over fire by a chain coming down from overhead. He motioned with his clenched fists like raising a flag.

I always worshiped our neighborhood's old-timers, but now I was more affirmed of the saintliness of their age. We're all being led to unsure fates, but here's a hero who never thought in terms of pleasure, insecure at times of even eating or where he'd live (in the Depression, he lost his home and grocery business he started at 3235 S. Princeton, and worked again at the building trades), who was being consoled with 3 more generations of Bozinovichs in their home at 2901 S. Princeton.

Oh, and there's more to his story: A St. Jerome's parishioner since the Parish's inception in 1912, a chronicler of our early community and its wood block streets, dirt sidewalks and horse-drawn streetcars, but George supersedes all that. His life is greater now, than those reminisces.

"Boss on top," he refers to the only reason for his inexplicable long life, "what God says, you listen to Him; you no can be boss."

His son Peter has already booked St. Jerome's Hall for Pa's 100th birthday next year, and George—who resembles Pat O'Brien or George Halas with thin, white hair and wizened years—is hindered only by weakening legs, probably from the burden of his long life.

And though his "happiness" may have been undefined to him, I'm sure there was some, just as we sense and glean from our everyday lives, from the tapestry of our surroundings that includes people such as him, from this setting that we can call the Neighborhood.

George and his wife, Mary and children.(Ca. 1923). Sons, Lawrence ,sitting on his knee, and Peter, standing (Deceased) ,and daughter, Anne, sitting (Deceased) .

(Both photos provided by son Lawrence aka "Larry ," a clear-minded , active 93. It`s all in the genes!)

George Bozinovich (1884-1984) . Neighborhood Croatian Patriarch . Here in his late 80`s . "Grand Marshall ," Saint Jerome`s Velika Gospa/ Feast of the Assumption , annual August 15th Parade.

By John Aranza 83

And About The Author

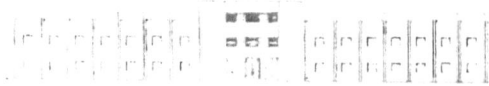

Balzekas Museum of Lithuanian Culture

6500 South Pulaski Road   Chicago, Illinois 60629   312 - 582-6500

Date: June 7, 1989
Contact person: Mildred Kletz
582-6500

FOR IMMEDIATE RELEASE

AN IN-DEPTH LOOK AT BRIDGEPORT

BRIDGEPORT: CHICAGO'S OLDEST NEIGHBORHOOD, is the title of an illustrated talk at the Balzekas Museum of Lithuanian Culture, 6500 S. Pulaski, on Sunday, June 25 at 2:00 P.M. Bridgeport resident and local historian, John Aranza, will discuss the colorful history of this neighborhood and its residents. Though best known as home to several of Chicago's mayors, Bridgeport has nurtured several generations of Irishmen, Lithuanians and other immigrant groups. Today the area is experiencing renewal and development. Mr. Aranza will examine the geography, landmarks, churches, and architectural diversity that help make Chicago's oldest neighborhood, Bridgeport, a historical and revitalized urban asset.

Aranza, whose family has lived in Bridgeport since 1906, has authored several newspaper articles on Chicago history and has appeared on Channel 7 talking on that topic. He is presently writing a history of De LaSalle High School, the school that Mayor Daley attended.

There is a $3 admission fee for the program. Refreshments will be served afterwards. Advance reservations are requested. Call 582-6500.

This program is sponsored in cooperation with the Chicago Gaelic Ancestry, a genealogical group that meets quarterly at the Newberry Library.

Real Est
• Apartments • Condos • I

Why I live here: Bridgeport

CITY LIVING
By John Aranza

Sometimes I wonder why I live in Bridgeport or anywhere in the Chicago area.

(Haven't you ever wondered why people who are born into the cold of Alaska, or the humidity of the Equator, don't leave for somewhere else?)

I've often asked myself that question, especially coming back to the neighborhood after a vacation. Our rows of rooftops look drab and monotonous, like Army bivouac pup tents.

But the neighborhood, which provides an intangible nurturing, like a plant that'll grow skyward toward the sun out of whatever mulch is underfoot, always will keep me here.

I'm 44, married for 22 years, and have one child, a son in sixth grade. I've lived most of my life in my parents' two-flat on South Parnell, and now in my own bungalow, a block away at the corner of 32nd and Parnell.

Bridgeport?

It isn't the simple boosterism that you see on the green and white "Welcome to Bridgeport" signs on 39th Street or Archer Avenue or 31st. They're like the Chamber of Commerce signs seen outside small towns everywhere.

It's not only the memory of our deceased mayor (Richard J. Daley) that leads people curiously here, like tourists climbing all over Mt. Olympus in Greece, looking for something.

I live here because my father emigrated from Yugoslavia—as did Lithuanian, Mexican, Irish, German, Polish, French, Italian, Swedish and Bohemian fathers—for that something better in life.

The director of Pulaski Savings on Morgan Street (an old-time Polish and Lithuanian business strip) lives among us on Lyman, not leaving for a far-away home each day. The family of Dr. Keith Knapp, who works at a prestigious medical center on 33rd and Halsted, live on Lowe Avenue, a neighborhood residential street.

Some people stay in this

> **" I live here because I know the families of the neighborhood children I see. "**

neighborhood for life. Dr. Jerry Schwartz, whose Bridgeport Medical Center is on 32nd and Wallace, once was the fountain clerk at the Modern Pharmacy at 31st and Wallace. Mike Nieman's son took over that pharmacy after his father's death.

I live here because I know the families of the neighborhood children I see. You'll recognize Richard M. Daley living among us; a Riccelli or a White or a Chodor will retain their family essence just as

Shakespeare's rose by any other name.

I live here because I walk among historical markers and legends not musty and staid, but changing with the times, somehow retaining a mysticism of what they were.

I pass brick garages protecting new Chrysler and Fords, buildings that I still remember from my childhood as housing peddlers' horses. And I stare up at the 4-by-4 beams protruding from the second story walls, where hay once was hoisted up into their lofts.

I'll pass St. Bridget's rectory on Archer Avenue with awe and pride, knowing it was once the Christian Brothers first assignment in Chicago, an Industrial School for boys in the 1860s (and also a home for displaced people after the Great Fire in 1871).

When my son and I make architectural digs along the Chicago River, near Archer and Ashland avenues, the beginnings of the Illinois and Michigan Canal, Bridgeport and really Chicago's history—I know we stand where Joliet

Turn to Page 13

SUN-TIMES/Rich Hein

John Aranza and his wife, Elaine, stand outside the bungalow in Bridgeport that they proudly call home.

By John Aranza 85

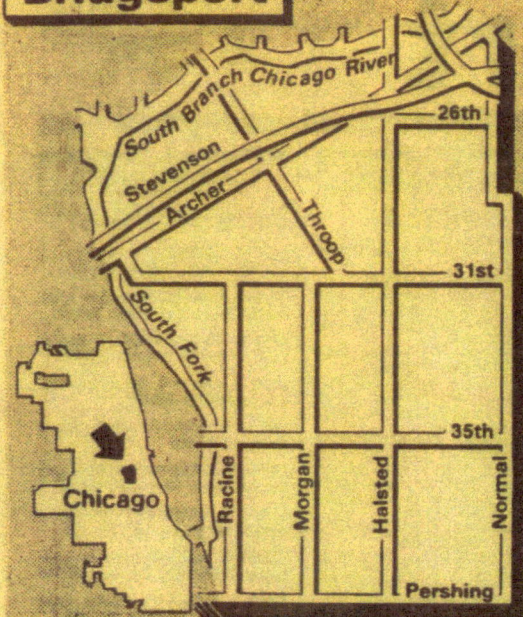

Bridgeport

SUN-TIMES/Rich Hein

LEFT: Bridgeport, known as the home of Chicago's most famous mayor, the late Richard J. Daley, is southwest of the Loop. ABOVE: Residents of Bridgeport have a variety of stores and restaurants to chose from, all within walking distance, near 35th and Halsted.

Why I live here: Bridgeport

Continued from Page 11
and Marquette did 300 before us, and I fantasize and palpitate probably just as excitedly.

And yet I know the actions of my neighborhood, home and birthplace sometimes seem scandalous to an outside world that magnifies them because of our political heritage.

Rather than cover up our blemishes and flaws, we try to do better, as we of Bridgeport know the truth and were taught to be truthful.

So harsh and happily can be Bridgeport's movements, not unlike the oceans of the world, brooding, storming, halcyon calm.

Laughing lunchtime workers in blood-stained frocks sit in front of the few remaining meat processing plants left from the Stockyard's heyday, at 38th and Halsted.
Babushka-wearing Lithuanian women walk from Lituanica Street, like time-travelers into modern society, to handle the vegetables in bushel baskets on the sidewalk in front of Tony's Supermarket on 32nd and Halsted.

And parents cheer for their Little League children in McGuane Park, their basketball-playing sons at De La Salle High School, or everyone's neighborhood team, the White Sox. (The Sox perform two blocks away in the adjacent community of Armour Square, thought of as part of Bridgeport.)

I'm going to a wake after I finish writing this. A neighborhood friend died, and the funeral is being held at Bridgeport Funeral Home on 31st and Parnell.

The funeral home is built on vacant lots where as small children Mickey and Danny Sheehan, Eddy Walz and his cousin J.R. and I played cowboys and Indians in that make-believe prairie Wild West.

A few things have changed in Bridgeport. Others have not. With all the neighborhood bars and tailors and shoe repairers and basement wine makers and open summer fire hydrants and quiet beer drinkers late on hot summer night front porches, the neighborhood is my home, my life.

Win $100, just for boasting

Readers are invited to submit letters on "Why I live here." Writers of each letter published will receive $100.

Letters should be 800 to 1,000 words and should be sent to: Homelife/Real Estate Section, The Chicago Sun-Times, 401 N. Wabash, Chicago 60611.

Please include a telephone number where you can be reached during the day.

Bridgeport-Armour Square: then, now, and the future?

Dear Editor:

Drive through most any rural Midwest farmland area and you'll find towns that were commercial centers in the 1800s. Usually, they were 20-to-30 miles apart, reached by wagon or carriage, flowering then withering if railroads or highways bypassed them.

Mid-state, Spencer, IN, is typical. A courthouse square with the World War 1 "Spirit of the American Doughboy" sculpture centering it. Modeled by native Indiana Ernest Moore Viquesney, it is the most copied statue in American history, replicated over 130 times. (One of them is inside the main gate 0 at Soldier Field.) Route 231 skips this "downtown" by two blocks, which could well have been 2,000 miles. And the malls and service stations on the outskirts of towns like these draw the lifesource—businesses and people—out of them.

Which brings to mind: what is the heart of Bridgeport-Armour Square? Our neighborhood is always likened to a little village. At one time the focal meeting place was David's Restaurant on the southwest corner of 31st and Halsted. The Maniates family expanded their ice cream parlor and candy shop into the Windy City Restaurant next door, becoming a large one themselves. Then they expanded south next to it creating the Governor's Table, one of our more elegant dining places. A fire, not rebuilding, and relocating to Arizona over 20 years ago darkenend that corner and that part of our lives. (Not to slight any one social gathering place, clubs like the Chi-Annies on 28th Place and Normal, the Gabric Boosters, still in existence on 29th and Princeton, pharmacies like Gabric's then called Balich Pharmacy on 31st and Wells, the Modern Pharmacy on 31st and Wallace, or Kunka Pharmacy on Archer and Loomis; the bowling alleys like Renzino's in Chinatown or Nap's on 26th and Normal; church societies - all these were meeting places too.)

The patriarchal symbol of the neighborhood was Richard J. Daley, of course. Few Chicagoans could boast of one of their own rising from common humbleness to Mayor of the city. Losing David's and the Mayor, long-time symbols, did create an uncertainty, however. We are undergoing a physical makeover of new homes and businesses, extending the life of the community. But what is our town square, so-to-speak? The center of our neighborhood? (A ride through powerful Congressman Dan Rostenkowski's Near Northwest Side ward during his years in office also wouldn't reveal the source of his power either or the backbone of the neighborhood. It was one reflecting our own—older homes, a few parks, unassuming commercial streets, churches; and his St. Stanislaus Kostka saved by veering the Kennedy expressway around it, like our St. Bridget's was spared.)

Our center isn't just one veteran's memorial revealing greatness like the Sintic playlot on 28th Place and Wallace or the Humbert playground on 31st and Lowe or the McKeon or Donovan Parks. It's not any one church or school or our many restaurants. It's the composite of all of these—shaped, formed, and sustained by our families and our family values. Families like the Garcias on Wallace Street, whose only concern and reason for being is their daughters and their education. Gudelia, the oldest, a valedictorian of Tilden, now attending college on a scholarship. Or the Carmonas on Lowe Avenue; what is more important than their children's education? We're represented by Dr. Knapp on 33rd and Halsted who was born, raised, and resides in the neighborhood. Jeff Sadowski, heading up the Valentine Boys and Girls Club.

Our heart and soul is held in the protective hands of all of these Bridgeport-Armour Square residents, most of whom were born and raised in the neighborhood: Lillian Buckley, principal of BCA South; Mary Ellen Ratkovich, Healy principal, of St. Jerome's Parish; Doreen Hurckes of St. Barbara's Parish; Geraldine Maratea, principal of her Santa Lucia Parish School; Mary Balich Vulich, teaching at Ward School; Dianne Geers, teaching at Lourdes Hall; these are just a few among the many, shaped by their principled parents, who now teach and guide others.

Many of us never needed more than what the neighborhood offered. The unspoken understanding of what the community is without a statue in a town square. All of them and you represent us. Who build our homes; shop our stores; walk our streets; attend our masses; and represent yourselves and us with the respect and dignity taught and learned through two and three generations of your families here.

Our only identifiable trait is that we generally know whose family you came from; and this shared recognition leads to mutual respect and community strength.

John E. Aranza

By John Aranza 87

I
wonder
if
the
world
can see
the
really truly ,
really
me

laughing
smiling
never
tears

hiding
sadness
doubts
fears

longing
searching
ever
reaching

why
this
never
ending
seeking

John ,
2000

88 My Bridgeport™

CHICAGO PROFILE / John Aranza

SUN-TIMES/Gene Pesek

HE IS

Writer, local history buff and De La Salle Institute grad.

RECENT BOOK

He conceived and wrote the centennial history of De La Salle Institute. The 160-page book is a tour de force, a sprightly history of the South Side high school and the city it serves.

ABOUT THE SCHOOL

De La Salle, at 3455 S. Wabash, was founded by the Christian Brothers in 1889 and continues to flourish. Five mayors are graduates, including the two Mayor Daleys.

STATS

Born, raised, lives in the Bridgeport neighborhood. Croatian descent. B.A. in English from DePaul. Now 50. Worked in the family business, John Aranza Real Estate & Insurance in Bridgeport. Late dad John founded it. Current day jobs: tour guide, scriptwriter, driver on Chicago Motor Coach buses.

BRIDGEPORT WIFE

Married 27 years to Elaine. Before they wed, "I always told her I'd marry a Bridgeport girl. She lived at Archer and Pulaski," which is *not* Bridgeport. "Then her mother told me she was born on Haynes Court over by St. Bridget's in Bridgeport!" Their son John Jr. is a De La Salle junior.

CAREER CHANGE

Five years ago, he decided to concentrate on writing. He started as an unpaid writer on the neighborhood newspaper, wrote for New City, U.S. Catholic, Neighborhood Works. Has had poems published, is writing two novels.

SPECIAL INTERESTS

He co-founded Save Our Sox. "I've played basketball with a group of friends, the Monday Night Basketball Association, since the 1950s. Even with Bobby Green, an MVP on the De La Salle football team."

PHILOSOPHY

"There really is a God. Wait long enough and he'll answer your prayers. It's not easy."
—Bob Herguth

Please feel free to contact me for additional copies, questions, comments or critiques at:

JohnAranza@sbcglobal.net
or call me at
(312) 842-7798

I want to hear from you!

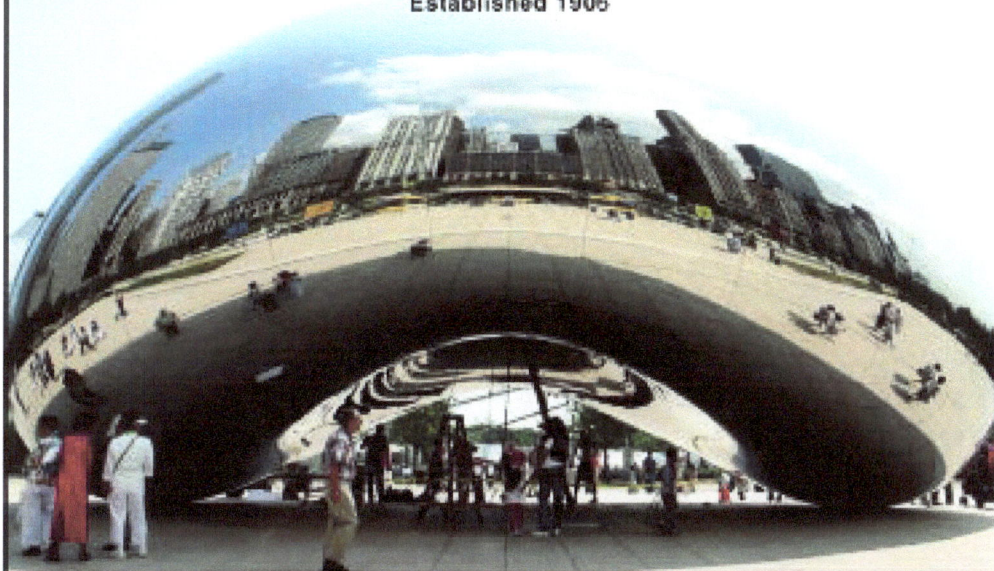

www.ingramcontent.com/pod-product-compliance
Lightning Source LLC
Chambersburg PA
CBHW061054090426
42742CB00002B/35

9780615677132